Portals to Cleansing

*Taking back your land
from the hands of the enemy*

Our homes, churches and other buildings are meant to be places of rest and security for us. *Portals to Cleansing* makes us aware when they are not, and how to cleanse and redeem them. As the warfare of the end-times increases, and tribulation is upon us, it becomes ever more crucial that especially our homes and church buildings remain clean places of rest and security. I recommend that every Christian who would be a workman who needs not to be ashamed make *Portals to Cleansing* a requisite portion of his study. Our families deserve to be at rest, safe in our Lord Jesus Christ.

John Loren Sanford
Co-Founder, Elijah House, Incorporated

Portals to Cleansing is one of the most exciting books I have ever read on this subject. It is much needed in a time of sharply increased demonic attack. Henry Malone has done an excellent job of applying biblical principles to spiritual issues. These biblical insights could save your health, family, marriage and finances as well as many other things too numerous to mention. My suggestion? Digest it and read it again and again!

John Paul Jackson
Founder, Streams Ministries International

Portals to Cleansing deals with issues too long ignored in the Church. This book provides believers with the insight and information necessary to maintain God's blessing and victory in their home and family.

Pastor Ken Hansen
Senior Pastor, Living Water Community Church
Bolingbrook, Illinois

Through deep biblical research, extensive experience and ministerial knowledge, Henry Malone imparts both revelation and insightful information. I highly recommend *Portals to Cleansing* as a great tool to equip every ministry.

Apostle John P. Kelly
President, LEAD and Ambassador Apostle for
International Coalition of Apostles

Many believers find their lives lacking in genuine freedom. I find the message in this book, *Portals to Cleansing* by Dr. Henry Malone, to be truthful and extremely practical for appropriating and reinforcing the victory over the devil that Christ gained for us. This is a liberating book.

Olen Griffing
Apostolic Pastor, Shady Grove Church
Grand Prairie, Texas

Portals to Cleansing is an ambitious book, sweeping in scope and biblical truths to bring people out of bondage and into restoration that they might be holy vessels unto the Lord. Henry Malone has effectively combined fresh insights with touching and candid illustrations in this biblically sound book. I highly recommend it.

Beth Alves
President, Intercessors International, Inc.

Portals to Cleansing

Dr. Henry Malone

Taking back your land
from the hands of the enemy

VISION
LIFE
PUBLICATIONS

Irving, Texas

First printing 2002
Second printing 2005
Third printing 2005
Fourth printing 2006

Request for information should be addressed to:
Vision Life Publications, P.O. Box 153691, Irving, Texas 75015
Email: info@visionlife.org Web site: http://www.visionlife.org

Unless otherwise noted, all Scripture quotations are taken from the *King James Version* and from *The Holy Bible, New King James Version*. Copyright 1979, 1980, 1982 by Thomas Nelson, Inc.

The incidents and illustrations recorded in this book are based on factual events. Some names and geographical locations have been changed to protect the identities of those involved.

ISBN -0-9717065-0-6
Designed by Ed Tuttle
Printed in the United States of America

I dedicate this book
to my beloved children and grandchildren—
the heritage of the Lord.
They are a blessing and a
source of encouragement to me.
They are my legacy.

To my daughter
Shaun Leslie Malone Shurey

To my son
Bart Alan Malone

To my daughter-in-law
Kimberley Bradley Malone

To my grandchildren
Daniel Christian Malone
Austin Gregory Malone
Hannah Grace Malone
Christopher Jayden Malone

Contents

Foreword   v

Acknowledgements   ix

Introduction   xi

One   Closed Doors—Open Portals

    1   Off Limits—No Trespassing   3
    2   Point of Entry—Doors to the Demonic   15
    3   No Intruders—Closing Doors   23
    4   A Dwelling Place—Habitation for Glory   31
    5   Portals—Entry Into the Supernatural   37

Two   Generation After Generation

    6   Curses—Truth and Consequences   47
    7   Cries From the Earth   57
    8   Paradigm of Pollution   69
    9   Deadly Obsessions   77
    10   Towers of Power   85

Three   Rules of Enforcement

    11   An Unbreakable Covenant   97
    12   Blood for Blood   103
    13   Recovery Operation   111
    14   Ground Zero—Cleaning Up   127

Four   Opening Portals

    15   Making Connection   135
    16   Two Are Better Than One   139
    17   Undefiled—Cleansing Your Home   143
    18   Marking Boundaries   151
    19   A Glorious Habitation   159

About the Author   163

Index   164

Vision Life Ministries   166

John Loren Sanford

We are in a war not of our choosing. We have chosen the Lord Jesus Christ as our Savior and Lord because He has first chosen us. His Kingdom is our home here, and heaven afterward. But another has chosen us as well. Satan does not want us to be at peace here nor to enter heaven hereafter. He cannot keep us from entering heaven if we have received Jesus as our Savior. But he can and does harass us and tries to prevent our homes, churches, work and play places from being a bit of heaven on Earth.

Unfortunately many believers, trusting that their safety depends solely on the Lord and requires nothing of them, have become naïve about our enemy's designs. Paul wrote many advices to the Corinthians, "...in order that no advantage be taken of us by Satan; for we are not ignorant of his schemes" (2 Corinthians 2:11). Henry Malone has been moved by the same loving concern of our Lord for the safety and well-being of His people. In *Portals to Cleansing*, Malone has taken much needed care for the protection of dwellings and lands from the inroads of Satan.

Portals to Cleansing begins by developing the history of mankind's defection from God in the Garden of Eden and subsequent events, showing how that has opened portals to the demonic even though salvation in Jesus has come. Throughout the book he reveals how five major portals grant to Satan and his hordes access to which otherwise they have no right—disobedience or willful sin, unforgiveness, inner vows and judgments, trauma and generational curses. These, he says, are countered by five portals to cleansing—repentance, redemption, restitution, restoration and reclamation.

Many Christians have been well aware of both fives. What is new, and desperately needed, is practical application, specifically about how places are infected and defiled. Christians suffer needlessly when demons are allowed inhabitation. Through biblical teaching and many stories, Henry Malone makes evident how our homes, church buildings and other places are defiled and what to do about that. He reveals how teams, under the guidance of the Holy Spirit, can discern both that evil is present and what has given the demonic access. He teaches carefully how to dispossess evil and reinstate heaven on Earth. After each teaching he suggests specific prayers, which he has written out for those who need them. Malone warns that these are not to become magic ritual incantations, but offers them as samples of the way each of us should pray in our own way.

Most importantly, Christians need to be made aware that things we have brought into our homes and other buildings may become invitations to the demonic. Deuteronomy 7:25-26 tells us we must not bring detestable things into our house, that abominable things are to be detested and destroyed with fire. Unfortunately, many have forgotten and many who remember are not aware which objects may be abominable. Henry Malone does the Body of Christ invaluable service by identifying specifically what ought not to be allowed to remain, and how to dispose of it. And also how to cleanse and redeem what does not need to be destroyed.

Our homes, churches and other buildings are meant to be places of rest and security for us. *Portals to Cleansing* makes us aware when they are not, and how to cleanse and redeem them. As the warfare of the end-times increases and tribulation is upon us, it becomes ever more crucial that especially our homes and church buildings remain clean places of rest and security. I recommend that every Christian who would be a workman who needs not to be ashamed make *Portals to Cleansing* a requisite portion of his study. Our families deserve to be at rest, safe in our Lord Jesus Christ.

John Loren Sanford
Co-Founder, Elijah House Incorporated

Acknowledgements

To my beloved wife, Tina. I could never do what I do without her. Thanks as always for your love, prayers, hard work and constant encouragement.

I also want to acknowledge those who have worked to make this book a reality. To Susan Martin, for her assistance with the researching and writing of this manuscript. My special thanks to Donna Hilton for her proofreading expertise. To my fellow warriors—the entire Vision Life Ministry team, for their prayers and encouragement throughout the entirety of this project.

Years ago, Hollywood released a movie called *The Amityville Horror*. The film told the story of a family who moved into a home in New England where all six members of the family were murdered. The house was later sold. Twenty-eight days after moving in, the new owners fled the home, terrorized by the demonic manifestations. They had just become the victims of what many call a "haunted house."

"Haunted house. Ridiculous! Demons aren't real. I don't believe that stuff." Well, I do believe. Let me tell you a story.

In the early 90s, my wife and I were going out of town on a ministry trip. A friend of mine Bishop William I. Daniels from Pakistan was visiting and needed a car to drive. So I lent him mine. It was a Toyota Corolla and even though we had bought it used, we had never had any trouble with it.

While in town, William was scheduled to speak at an Arlington church. He was to meet with the pastor, Wayne Kenyon, 30 minutes before the service to talk and pray together. On Sunday, instead of showing up early, he arrived 40 minutes late. By the time he arrived, the service had already started. He told Wayne that on the way to church, my car had almost come to a stop three times–accelerating to 60 mph and then abruptly dropping to 15 mph. He had barely escaped a serious accident three times as 18-wheelers skidded within inches of his bumper. Wayne told him they would go ahead with the service, have lunch afterward, and then find a garage to repair my car. He assured William that everything would be OK.

The service went well and afterward they decided to go to a local restaurant for lunch. Wayne told William to follow him. He started out of the parking lot leaving William behind. William started the car, but the transmission failed and the car wouldn't move.

When Wayne got to the first stop sign, he realized that William wasn't following him so he turned around and went back to the church. There he found William still sitting in the parking lot. Certain that he could get my car going, Wayne gave William the keys to his truck and told him that he would meet him at the restaurant.

William pulled out of the parking lot and onto the service road heading toward the freeway. The service road was about 18 feet wide and had a high bank on the left side. Beyond the bank was a large, heavily wooded area with very high trees. William was halfway down the road when suddenly two figures flashed before him on both sides of the steering wheel.

They appeared to him as Arabic men and were dressed all in black with turbans covering their heads. They immediately took control of the wheel. The truck turned off the road. The wheels were spinning, leaving dark black tire marks on the road. The marks ended abruptly at the line of grass along the service road. But the truck was nowhere in sight.

While all of this was happening to William, Wayne had finally gotten my car to move and was now on the service road. He was puzzled by the fact that, even though not much time had passed, he couldn't see William or his truck anywhere. While he was still looking for William, a truck driver got his attention and flagged him down. He told Wayne that he and his partner had been driving their 18-wheeler down the freeway when they saw a truck leave the service road, fly through the air and crash just beyond the tree line.

Certain that William was dead or in need of immediate emergency treatment, Wayne and the truck driver walked up the embankment. They made their way through the wooded area and found the truck, 265 feet beyond the tree line. William was inside, passed out on the seat. While Wayne stayed with William, the truck driver left to call 9-1-1 and the Texas troopers.

Help arrived shortly. Rescue crews began the difficult task of cutting through the dense woods to get to William. They found many large broken tree limbs that had been hit by the truck as they made their way closer to the crash scene. Finally they reached William, pulled him from the truck, put him on a stretcher and transported him to the closest emergency room. The emergency room staff examined William, but was amazed to find only a small bruise on his right leg.

When they had completed their examination, a Texas trooper interviewed William regarding the accident. He asked him, "How did this happened? Do you remember how your truck ended up in the woods? William had only one answer. He told the trooper about the two demonic figures—the Arabic men, dressed in black that had appeared in the truck and taken control of the steering wheel. The trooper just happened to be a Christian and believed William, but told him in no uncertain terms, "I can't put that in my report. Austin, Texas would never believe it." Instead, the trooper had another idea, "Let's just say, you don't know how you got there."

For the trooper the case was closed. But many questions remained. Why had my car malfunctioned? What was behind the demonic spirits who had taken control of Wayne's truck and tried to kill William? Answers were on the way.

When William was released from the emergency room, he and Wayne went to a home where several church intercessors had gathered to pray when they received word of the accident. Overjoyed to see William unhurt, they continued to pray for the reason behind the accident. As they continued, one of the intercessors got a prophetic word. She saw someone in William's family cursing him.

Her words struck a cord in William. He remembered that the night of his ordination, a member of his family had said, "You will never live to complete the work to which you have been called." The word of knowledge answered the questions as to why William had seen the two demonic figures and why they had tried to kill him. Unfortunately, the curse would continue to follow William. Shortly after the accident he was diagnosed with pancreatic cancer that later would result in complete liver failure. He died at the age of 46, never completing all God had called him to do.

The story didn't end there. There were still more unanswered questions. When Tina and I returned home from our ministry trip, we picked up our car at Wayne Kenyon's church. I took the car to a mechanic. He put in what would end up being the first of five transmissions. None of them every lasted over a week. Each time all but the lowest gears were damaged. After months of replacing transmission after transmission, my mechanic refused to do any more replacements. I searched for the answer to the question: Why was my car cursed? I was about to get the answer.

Tina and I had a dear friend visiting us from out of town. She is a seer with a powerful prophetic gift, so we asked her to see what God would show her. After praying for some time she said, "I see two black balls on a string with orange and yellow dots and three more of these in the glove compartment." She told us that the black balls were positioned behind the firewall where the heater and the water connection go back into the engine. We went to our driveway, opened the hood of the car and found the objects exactly where she described. There were two black balls under the hood and three more in the glove compartment. I removed them, broke the curses attached to them and my car, and smashed them into pieces with a hammer.

Although I never knew how the items got into my car, most of the questions had been answered. The trouble with my transmission was over. Never again would I have that problem. All was well. My experience had confirmed what I already knew—the demonic isn't some Hollywood special effect or top-grossing movie. It's real and it affects people everywhere.

Since the summer of 1973, when God first thrust me into the realm of the supernatural, I have seen into the unseen. I have been in houses that in one way or another were "haunted." Demons had taken up residence, and the owners didn't know what to do. Over the years, I've encountered people from every walk of life, who have sought my help in cleansing their property, homes, possessions and even, in some cases, their pets. I have seen some pretty unusual things over the years as Satan has fought for control of what he thought was "his territory." But each time God has moved in a mighty way to bring deliverance and freedom. At the end of the battle, instead of being captives in their own home, those that received ministry and a touch from God were free to enjoy the peace and joy which comes when God's presence fills a place and makes it His habitation.

Even though I have been cleansing houses for 29 of the last 41 years of ministry, God has just recently given me new revelation regarding the power of His body and blood. Jesus is in the business of freedom. If you've read the book *Shadow Boxing* or attended one of my seminars, you know that I believe Jesus came to set the captives free. Luke 4:18 says, "The Spirit of the Lord is upon Me, Because He has anointed Me To preach the gospel to the poor; He has sent Me to heal the brokenhearted, To proclaim liberty to the captives And recovery of sight to the blind, To set at liberty those who are oppressed." Jesus wants us to be free! He wants us to dwell in peace in our homes and have victory over all the power of the enemy in every area of our lives. That's exactly what He purchased for us—total and complete freedom.

Freedom is ours through the body and blood of Jesus. Communion is a tangible sign of our eternal covenant with God. It's the signpost to the powers of darkness that we are "off limits" to Satan's interference in our lives and homes. His body and blood saves us, heals us, brings provision and insures our protection. It brings the power to cleanse our property, homes, possessions and pets. I know because I've seen it happen time and time again. Jesus has given each of us the power and authority to put His blood, His body and His

Name into action to free our land and possessions.

This book is about God's original intention for the earth. It's about God's ownership, and man's dominion and authority. The world we see today doesn't look like what God created. It has become polluted and defiled. The shedding of innocent blood has brought curses to the land. Idolatry and rebellion have opened the earth to Satan and his authority. But there is a way to remove the curses that run from generation to generation. There is a portal, a doorway, for God to bring freedom and cleansing.

During the rest of this book, you'll learn the foundation for cleansing, what man did to lose his authority, how Satan took control of the earth, and why curses have created a demonic portal. I'll show you how to take back all the enemy has stolen from you and share personal case studies that illustrate how strongholds get a foothold in our homes and lives. You'll find out how to remove obstacles to freedom and learn what steps you need to follow to take back your land from the hands of the enemy.

I believe with all of my heart that by the time you've reached the last page, you'll be ready to fight for what's really yours and the freedom of all you possess. As you go to battle, it's my prayer that you and your household will experience freedom that will make your home a place of habitation where God's Spirit dwells in peace, praise, joy and protection.

Part One

Closed Doors—
Open Portals

Chapter 1

Off Limits—
No Trespassing

Septembember 11, 2001, when enemies of the United States of America declared war against freedom and struck a blow to the heart of the nation, we wondered what life would be like without the ever-present influence of Satan, his demonic hordes, sin, sickness and, worst of all, death. We wished we could roll back time to the Garden of Eden and help Adam and Eve put up a permanent "NO TRESSPASSING" sign on the earth. We prayed that we could seal off our borders from the destruction that came with the choices they had made. Yet we have made them too.

All of our lives, each of us has chosen to close or open doors to Satan, giving him legal right to destroy us. We have even given his forces of darkness squatter's rights to the earth, the nations, the cities and our individual homes. He has stepped through the crack in the door that we have given him and walked right in and claimed adverse possession. It all sounds legally binding, and it is.

Squatters Are Not Tenants

In the realm of property rights, natural law has some interesting precedents with clear spiritual applications. Let's deal with the actual law first. Squatters' rights are a recognized means, in property law, of taking possession without an agreement from the landlord. Squatters simply move in and create the appearance of being tenants. Even though they pay nothing and do not have permission to stay on the property, they continue to possess the land. They can stay for a short time or a longer period. They are legally "trespassers," but because the owner or landlord has made no complaint against them, they cannot be removed. Not even the police can arrest and remove them without a formal complaint. The longer the squatter stays, the more difficult it is for the legal owner or landlord to take back the land.

The Tactics of Squatters

Squatters use some interesting tactics. They look for a potential property. They wait for an opportunity. They move in and adapt to the neighborhood. They fit into the surroundings. They move in and bring their possessions. They make it look like it is their home even when it isn't. Just ask one minister and his wife how quickly trespassers can turn into squatters.

> They started feeling a strange presence in the house. Ellie was often jerked awake in the middle of the night by an unseen force.

For Barry and his wife, Ellie, it was the worst time of their lives. They had come to a Northern California valley town to help a senior pastor and his wife with their small church. It wasn't their first assignment. They had been in the ministry for many years. At first things went well. The church was growing, people were getting saved, and others were getting free from drugs and alcohol. Then an alarming pattern started. In less than a week their son Jeremy, who was visiting from Southern California, had to be rushed to the hospital with an irregular heartbeat. Barry was nearly injured in an automobile accident. He also fell and injured his knee while working at home.

Ellie too barely escaped an automobile accident. All of this happened in one short week.

A Strange Presence

Then they started feeling a strange presence in the house. Ellie was often jerked awake in the middle of the night by an unseen force. Both Barry and Ellie had seen strange markings on the ground. Twigs and rocks and strange "Y" symbols. They frequently heard noises at night around the windows. They felt as if someone were constantly watching them.

Knowing that something had to be done and feeling that witchcraft might be involved, Barry heard of our ministry and called us. He asked if we could send a team out to investigate and then cleanse their home.

Two of our team volunteered for the assignment and went out on a Saturday evening. Several of Barry and Ellie's intercessors from the church also showed up to pray. They all took communion and began to pray. As they did, God began to reveal a strategy for the cleansing. They took anointing oil and walked the property line, pouring out the anointing oil and praying a hedge by the authority of the blood of Jesus.

When some of the team reached the area of the back bedroom they sensed that something was concentrated in that area. They went inside, but got no release. They returned outside and decided to crawl underneath the house to the corner of the bedroom. At the exact corner underneath the house, they found a brick altar, a triangular piece of wood, and a stone plaque with the markings of a snake on it. As they began to dismantle the altar, a word of knowledge came to dig underneath. When they did, they found pieces of different kinds of bones where a sacrifice had been made. They removed all of the items and returned to the outside of the house.

At the outside corner of the house nearest the bedroom, they discovered five black feathers placed equal distance from each other around the base of a large tree. A sixth matching black feather pointed to the bedroom window. Still more feathers pointed to the crawl space door. Around the other areas of the yard were three pronged branches, horizontal rock patterns, more black feathers and burned areas.

Clearly, a witch coven had targeted Barry and Ellie's house. But this would not be the end of the attacks on their property.

An Upside Down Cross

Months later they asked a friend to help them repair a leak in the roof. The section of roof was right above the room they often used for ministry. Several weeks later their friend called to set up a time to finish his work. He remarked to Barry, "Hey man, the cross you have on your roof is pretty cool!"

"What cross?" Barry asked.

"The big white cross that's on the roof."

As soon as he got off the phone, Barry and Ellie checked out the roof. Much to their surprise, a large, upside down cross filled the entire section of the roof. They hadn't painted it. The question was: Who had?

Once again, strange incidents started to occur. More signs were left. A darker presence filled the house. Barry called our ministry again.

The same team members went back out to the property. They found other places where someone had tried to go underneath the house. They discovered a partial altar including a board, triangle and stones underneath the house. It was barely visible above the standing water of recent rains. Around the exterior of the house and all throughout the yard there were black feathers, stones and "Y" patterns. All appeared to be indicators of coven activity.

Once again the team prayed and anointed the house. Barry and Ellie had their friend paint over the cross on the rooftop. For a while things returned to normal, but not for long.

Over the next 10 months, night after night and week after week, the demonic harassment continued. Sometimes the attacks were so severe that it forced Barry and Ellie to leave their own home and seek safety at the home of friends. Especially during satanic holidays and rituals, they feared for their lives. Many nights, dark celestial figures projected into their bedroom. During the daytime, when they were gone, someone broke in and stole their house keys and car keys.

The police did nothing. There was no one to help them but God.

They continued to pray and believe. Even though they were constantly harassed, God protected their lives from the destruction of the enemy. Barry placed another call to the ministry for help.

The Power of Communion

This time I went with a team of six from the ministry. Several large gallon jars of anointing oil were blessed and then we poured it along the property lines until all the boundaries of the land had been covered. We gathered together and stood in a circle to observe communion. (Note: You may find that your particular beliefs, theology or denominational position are not in agreement with what I will share regarding communion. It has been my experience that this particular observance brings with it tremendous anointing and the power to release and reclaim the land. I recognize the different beliefs regarding the blessing and observance of communion, and the sanctity and reverence for the elements. Please feel free to observe and practice only what you are comfortable with.)

> The earth was redeemed. It was "bought back." It belongs to God! But we must force the enemy off the land.

I took a whole loaf of bread representing the body of Jesus and blessed it and observed communion. A hole was dug, the remainder of the bread placed in it. Then I took the fruit of the vine. I poured it over the same area and declared the land cleansed by the blood of Jesus. I prayed and reclaimed the ground, declaring it whole and complete by the body of Jesus. Everyone sensed the tangible anointing of God. We felt a mighty release of God's Spirit as we by faith appropriated the once-for-all sacrifice of the blood of Jesus.

When Jesus was dying on the Cross, the very moment the first drop of His perfect blood fell to the earth, the earth was redeemed. It was "bought back." It belongs to God! But we must force the enemy off the land. I believe that this observance of communion can be a powerful means of bringing the power to cleanse, reclaim and recover the land through the body and blood of Jesus.

The victory was won. The battle had been hard fought. Barry and Ellie had learned a valuable spiritual lesson. The enemy of our souls is relentless. Satan is always looking for just the right opportunity to harass us. He finds moments to intrude into our lives. He takes every advantage he can. Sometimes he uses an open door into our lives. Maybe we've forgotten to lock a door—willful sin, unforgiveness, inner vows, trauma, generational curses. Maybe it's an attitude, an object or even a relationship. It doesn't matter. Any door will do.

Once he gets control, he can easily become a "spiritual squatter" and eventually take possession of our lives. He, like a physical squatter, is betting that you will never file a complaint and evict him. He's hoping we don't notice he's there. He wants to take full possession.

No Trespassing

Squatters often move on to the next step of possession. If they can stay long enough, they can actually exclude the right of the owner to the land. They can gain full ownership via adverse possession after a period of 12 years if the owner refuses to make a complaint, abandons the land, or in any way refuses to claim ownership. (Note: The legal time period for adverse possession varies from state to state.)

We have authority as believers to take possession of our lives and to ensure that Satan and the forces of darkness do not take up residence and claim squatters rights by adverse possession. When we fail to use our authority and demand Satan's eviction from our lives, homes, cities and nations, he gains greater access to our lives and builds strongholds. The longer Satan's strongholds are in place, the more difficult it becomes to remove them, repair the damage, and renew our strength from the battle.

We must not abandon our lives to Satan and his demons. We must be determined to guard against his on-going attempts to get a foothold, build a stronghold, and lay siege to the property that is our lives. We must walk the boundaries, put up the fences, and post "NO TRESPASSING" signs on our hearts, lives, homes, and possessions.

The Judgment of God

Do not take lightly the judgment that comes when we allow Satan and his demonic forces to trespass in our lives, cities and nations. In Leviticus 18:26-28 God says, "You shall therefore keep My statues and My judgments, and shall not commit any of these abominations, either any of your own nation or any stranger who dwells among (for all these abominations the men of the land have done, who were before you, and thus the land is defiled), lest the land vomit you out also when you defile it, as it vomited out the nations that were before you."

What was it in these verses that has so stirred the anger of God's judgment? These five things: **incest** (Leviticus 18:6-19), **adultery** (Leviticus 18:20), **divination**, (Leviticus 18:21), **homosexuality** (Leviticus 18:22) and **bestiality** (Leviticus 18:23). Every nation of the earth, including America, should take note. We are guilty of all these and God says our land is defiled.

The Battle Is the Lord's

We are in a war. The battle is the Lord's, but we are the warriors of the spirit. Each of us must put on our armor, stand our post, and take our place with other believers "as more than conquerors." Jesus has given us His Name and His authority with which to fight. God has put us in the time and place He wants us to live. He has determined not only when we live, but where, down to the country, state, neighborhood and street. God knew our exact address before we did.

John Paul Jackson puts it this way: "To Adam, it was the Garden of Eden. To Abraham and Moses, it was the Promised Land which they knew not, but to which they journeyed. To Elijah, it was the wilderness and the brook Cherith. To Esther, it was Shushan or Babylon. To Ruth, it was Bethlehem. To Nehemiah, it was Jerusalem. To Jacob, it was Bethel. And to the 120, it was the Upper Room."

The place we call "home," with its geography, longitude and

latitude, is a place where God wants to walk, accomplish His purposes, talk to the people of the earth, and fulfill His destiny. God wants our habitations to become His habitation. Each of us has a specific geographic place, or as John Paul Jackson puts it, "land of anointing," that we can impact for the kingdom of God. Where you live will not only impact you, but you will impact and shape it.

If you are an American, ask yourself, "Where was I prior to September 11, 2001? Was I armed and ready in the realm of the spirit? Did I leave my personal land unguarded? Did the trespassers in my life leave my city and nation open for the larger assault? Did the squatters take adverse possession right under my nose?"

No matter what your national heritage or ethnicity, you, as a believer, can make a difference and take back the land. As Americans, we know now that the terrorists who came to destroy our nation from within were hidden. We didn't notice them because they looked too much like us. They blended in, adapted to their surroundings, and made us think they were "just like us." They were squatters who had planned an adverse possession of our land.

Take Back Your Land

Decide in your own life, home and family that you won't be caught off guard. Determine to take back the land of your life and the property and possessions God has given you. Don't let Satan pull off a surprise attack. Don't let him catch you off guard by allowing the familiar to lure you into the comfortable. Don't let the demonic squatters fool you with the appearance of "normalcy." Allow God to fence you in by His Spirit and draw your boundary lines. Walk the property lines of your life and declare it off limits to trespassers and squatters. Don't let Satan take adverse possession of your life and home. Take back the land.

> Decide that you won't be caught off guard. Determine to take back the land of your life and the property and possessions God has given you.

That's exactly what a local church did. In the spring of 1997, the church's intercessors began searching for reasons why the congregation could never fully experience the sustained presence of God. They would often ride a wave of the Spirit only to drop back to where they were before. Each time, the church experienced more and more frustration. In addition, a kind of stinginess affected the congregation. Finances were in short supply. There never was quite enough. They knew God wanted to do something powerful in their church, but there was an unseen obstacle preventing them from moving forward. But what was it?

One Church's Breakthrough

By the summer, several of the intercessors had decided to research the history of the community and the property. What they discovered would prove to be very interesting and the key to their breakthrough.

Used by mutual agreement between the Indians and the military in the mid-1700s, the land was designated as an "Indian boundary." The Indians agreed to allow the military to use the land as an outpost. The two parties lived together in peace.

In 1794, the United States military broke their agreement. Out of greed, they acquired the land by force and added to a growing landmass held in the West by the United States. In the middle of the night they came in, slaughtered the men, women and children, and took the land. Because of their actions, the land received a curse. Greed motivated the shedding of innocent blood. The land on which the church plant was built was defiled.

A week later, the pastors met a Native American Indian. He had been traveling the country helping churches to conduct Identificational Repentance Ceremonies to cleanse the land where atrocities had been committed against the nation's first landholders. He helped the church to conduct a service of confession and repentance.

The week after the service, the church experienced its first breakthrough. They began their capital stewardship campaign to raise $300,000 to pay off the mortgage and pave the way for additional construction.

In previous weeks, the giving had averaged only $4800. Starting the next Sunday, giving rose to $8,000. Today, giving has not only reached $16,000 per week, but the church has grown from 300 to 700. They went over their goal of $300,000 with an extra $420,000. The activities center they hoped to build turned from a $400,000 facility into a $1.4 million complex. By March 2001, over four years later, their second stewardship campaign began to raise $1 million for a new 1,000 seat sanctuary and a 30,000 square foot educational center. With two weeks left in the campaign they had already raised $1.5 million. The curse was gone. The breakthrough had definitely come.

You can experience the same thing by taking hold of God's anointing for the land on which you live and the city you inhabit. When you are in God's will and are in the place to which He has sent you, there will be a strong anointing of faith to impact the people around you. You will have favor. You will have good success and take back the land. You will be the light that shines brightly in the darkness. Commit today to take back the land. Be more than a conqueror in the place that God has called you.

> Lord Jesus. I refuse to be the victim of Satan's sneak attack. I ask You to help me to identify any area of "spiritual trespassing" where Satan has gotten a foot in the door and has begun to establish a foothold. Destroy any and all strongholds in my life that have given Satan a prime opportunity to attack me and take possession of my mind, will, emotions, body and decisions. In the Name of Jesus, I evict all demonic forces from my mind, will, emotions, body, decisions and life. I take authority over the physical property and possessions You have given me and declare "NO TRESPASSING" to Satan and his demons. I put on the full armor of God and choose to enter the battle. Thank You, God, that You have already won the battle for my family, my home, my city, my nation and me. Help me to be more than a conqueror and to give "no place" to the evil one. Amen.

Chapter 2

Point of Entry—
Doors to the Demonic

They're here," the famous line from the 1982 horror movie *Poltergeist* served as an announcement of the presence of demonic spirits. He was knocking on doors looking for a way in. Today he's here, still knocking, still looking for a way in. He's found it via cable, satellite, movies, video games, magazines, books and children's toys. The door has been left ajar and Satan has just walked into the homes of millions.

With little to no resistance he and his demonic forces have taken up residence and feel quite comfortable in neighborhoods and cities around the world. Some don't even know he's moved in. Others have become so desensitized by his presence that they can't tell the difference anymore between light and darkness and the shadows in between. Sadly, many of them are believers.

Signposts of Your Heart

Perhaps you remember a time when the door of your soul was locked. Jesus was alive and well in your life. Satan's entry was prohibited. The signposts on your heart read, "NO TRESPASSING." Little by little you started to give the enemy a point of entry. Maybe it was the day you purchased a satellite system that gave you access to hundreds of channels. Then one night when the children and your wife were in bed, you decided to purchase a pay-per-view movie—not one of the blockbuster hits, but an "adult" film. "I'm just curious. One look won't hurt anything," you thought. It soon led to other things.

Possibly it came the day you picked up a ladies magazine at the grocery store. The seductive images and tantalizing stories caught your attention. Things had been a little dull lately, even boring. You needed some excitement and you got it. Things stirred inside you, but you didn't know how to stop them.

Then there was the afternoon you dropped your child's backpack. Pokemon cards and a Harry Potter book tumbled onto the floor. "Where did that come from?" you asked yourself. Then you remembered the weeks of allowance that your son had been saving for something special. Like the many other things in your household, they had opened a door to the dark side that now would not easily be shut. Satan started with a foot in the door that step by step led to a stronghold. The enemy had set up camp. Getting rid of the enemy would mean all-out war.

Tormenting Fear

They had just purchased a beautiful home in a wooded area in the East. Life was good. Steven's 3-year-old business was going well and new clients were coming in on a daily basis. His wife, Katie, was expecting their third child in the fall, a boy. They already had two girls, twins, Heather and Amy. Both were doing fine, except for one thing: They had nightmares and severe episodes of tormenting fear which left them totally traumatized.

It had become difficult, if not impossible, to get them to sleep each night. Their health had also become a concern. They had developed chronic bronchitis that had landed both of them in the hospital on more than one occasion, most recently sending them to ICU.

Two of our team went to the house to do a cleansing. They all stood in the kitchen and took communion together and prayed. Then the team began walking through the house. Little seemed to surface until they reached the children's wing. Suddenly a perverted, dark presence surrounded them. It only worsened as they made their way into the playroom and then escalated as they ended up in the bedroom.

They cleansed the hallway and playroom taking authority over every spirit of perversion, whoredom and jealousy, including anger and abuse. They also cleansed the bathroom that was between the playroom and the bedroom. Finally they walked back into the bedroom. They both noticed the wallpaper. It had cartoon figures on it, but their eyes seemed to draw the teams' attention. It was almost as if the eyes of the characters followed them.

> Suddenly a perverted, dark presence surrounded them. It only worsened as they made their way into the playroom and then escalated, as they ended up in the bedroom.

The husband, who had been escorting them through the house, mentioned that the wing was the only area of the house they hadn't redecorated. The wallpaper had been selected and hung by the prior owner. The team began to pray, breaking the spirits of fear, torment and violence in the room. Then they broke the spirits attached to the cartoon characters. They anointed all of the walls and the wallpaper. The team recommended that the wallpaper should be removed and the walls repainted. The husband and wife agreed.

The team continued through the rest of the house, suggesting that some other items in the attic be removed as well. They prayed for each member of the family and then blessed the house and left.

The next day, one of the team got an urgent call. Katie had hired several people to come and remove the wallpaper and repaint all the rooms in the children's wing. No matter what they used they could not remove all of the wallpaper and they had put more than three coats of paint on the walls and it still didn't cover the paper.

The team member went back out to the house, prayed, took authority over the situation and left with peace restored to the household. The painters continued their work without any further trouble. The room no longer caused Heather and Amy any trouble and the family has received a new addition to their family, a son and a baby brother, Gabriel Max.

Winning the War

This wasn't the only family that's had to learn how difficult it is to win the war against the forces of darkness. Any military strategist will tell you that it's easier to maintain the peace than win a war. First Peter 5:8 declares, "Be sober, be vigilant; because your adversary the devil walks about like a roaring lion, seeking whom he may devour." Satan has one battle plan—your destruction. He is constantly looking for any door of opportunity which gives him a way to establish a foothold, then a stronghold and finally your destruction. The only way you can avoid his onslaught is to be sober and vigilant, and make a decision to be watchful and diligent in the things of God.

The *Wuest* translation of 1 Peter 5:8 reads this way, "Be of a sober mind, be watchful. Your adversary who is a slanderer, namely the devil, as a lion roaring in fierce hunger, is constantly walking about, always seeking someone to be devouring." Verse 9 continues, "Stand immovable against his onset, solid as a rock in your faith, knowing that the same kind of sufferings are being accomplished in your brotherhood which is in the world."

> God expects each of us to close the doorways in our lives that have given Satan and his demonic forces a point of entry and a place of habitation.

God expects each of us to close the doorways in our lives that have given Satan and his demonic forces a point of entry and a place of habitation. Not only are we to be the spiritual dwelling place of God, but also our physical homes and the property that has been given to us are to be places where God is exalted, his presence is felt and his power is displayed.

Dedicated to God

In Jewish tradition, a mezuzah, the Hebrew word for doorpost, was fastened to the upper right-hand part of the outside door of each home as a sign of obedience and dedication to God. The word "mezuzah" comes from the root "zuz" which means turning oneself about and refers to that place on the door where the hinges turn. The word is translated in Exodus 12:7 as a "side-post" and in Exodus 21:6 and Deuteronomy 6:9 as "posts." The actual mezuzah is a symbol of faith and is a wooden, glass, ceramic or metal case roughly two to six inches in length. Inside is a rectangular piece of parchment with Hebrew scriptures written on it by hand in ink. The word for God, Shaddai, appears on the back of the parchment and is visible at the top of the mezuzah when it is affixed to the doorpost.

When the mezuzah is placed on the posts of the door, it is done in obedience to the command, "Thou shalt write them (the words of the law) upon the posts of thy house, and on thy gates" (Deuteronomy 6:9). After 4,000 years of tradition, it is still a reminder that every home must be sanctified, kept free from evil and protected by the blood of the lamb.

Practicing Jews would never think of entering or leaving their home without placing the fingertips of their right hand on the mezuzah, touching their lips and saying, "May God keep my going out and my coming in from now and forevermore" (Psalm 121:8).

This prayer of David daily serves as recognition of God's divine presence and protection on their home. In fact, Jewish people today still practice the custom of dedicating their homes. Ruth Specter Lacelle tells of the dedication ceremony in her book *Jewish Faith and the New Covenant*. The ceremony, called the "Hanukat Habayit," is recorded in Deuteronomy 20:5 and Psalm 30 and begins with the fastening of the mezuzah on the doorpost. A blessing is recited: "Blessed art thou, O Lord, our God, King of the Universe, Who hast

made us holy with thy commandments and hast commanded us to
fasten the mezuzah." Then a prayer follows: "Master of the Universe,
look down from Thine holy habitation and accept in mercy and favor
the prayer of Thy children who are here gathered to dedicate this
dwelling and to offer their thanksgiving. Grant them that they may live
in their homes in brotherhood and friendship."

Doorways of the Heart

For believers, God commands us to write His Word on our hearts.
Deuteronomy 6:4-6 says, " Hear, O Israel: The Lord our God, the Lord is
one! You shall love the Lord your God with all your heart, with all your
soul, and with all your strength. And these words which I command you
today shall be in your heart." As Ruth Specter Lacelle says, "It is more
important to have the Word of God fixed in the heart than to have it
wrapped up in a small box and nailed to the door of a house!"

Believers have the constant reminder of the protection of the
Lamb of God Who applies His blood to our hearts. He watches over
us. He is always with us. He is our protector as we come into our
homes and as we go out from our homes. This is all the more reason
for every believer to guard the doorway to his heart and home from
the presence of evil.

Begin, right now, to ask the Holy Spirit to reveal to you any defiling
things to which you have opened a door in your life and home.

Lord Jesus, forgive me for not guarding my heart and my home
from Satan and the powers of darkness. I repent of allowing him
into my thinking, attitudes and actions. Forgive me for allowing
Satan to create a foothold and build a stronghold in my life.
Forgive me for walking so close to the line of evil and so far away
from that which is right in Your eyes. Forgive me for seeking
darkness rather than Your light. Help me, Holy Spirit, to identify
those areas in my life that need to change. Show me the things
that have come into my home that need to be removed,
destroyed or cleansed so that I can live in freedom. Lord Jesus,

I want my life to be a dwelling place for You, and my home to be a place of habitation for Your presence, peace and power. Come and take me from darkness and the shadows and put me into a place of light with You. Help me to be sober, vigilant and diligent so that I can stand against the roaring lion who seeks to devour and destroy me. Thank You Lord, for bringing me to freedom, for removing darkness from my heart, for giving me the power to stand against the enemy, and for filling my heart and life with Your presence and protection. Amen.

Chapter 3

No Intruders—
Closing Doors

O pen doors invite intruders. A friend told me a story not too long ago about a couple they knew who activated their home security system, only to return later that night to find their home not exactly the way they left it. The furniture was all in its place. No stereo equipment was missing. Computers and valuables were all intact.

Yet something was different. They sensed it immediately when they exited their car and walked in through the garage.

As they walked into the hallway and into the living area, they noticed a chair out of place in the kitchen. It was pulled away from the table as if someone had sat there for a moment. They looked at each other and then began slowly making their way through the house checking every room. As the husband investigated upstairs, the wife checked the back door. It was closed, but unlocked. They both knew someone had walked into their home.

Later they found the tag the local policeman had left. After a brief call they discovered that an officer had responded to their alarm and discovered the back door wide open. He had sat down at the table to do his report after calling the alarm company. Alarm systems are great. They make a lot of noise when someone enters a protected zone. Still they're no match for the intruder who walks in through a back door left unlocked.

Unlocked Doors

Satan uses the unlocked doors of our lives to his advantage and sends in his demonic forces to get what they can before we decide to exercise our authority. As you cleanse your house and close every door to the enemy, make sure that you secure the locks and keep the keys somewhere he can't find them.

Every house cleansing is different because just like every person, every home has a story, history, personality and its own problems. Keep in mind that there are no hard and fast rules for cleansing a house, but there are some guidelines. Be

> Satan uses the unlocked doors of our lives to his advantage and sends in his demonic forces to get what they can.

sensitive to the Holy Spirit and obey His instructions. What He tells you to do should always line up in concept, principal and practice with the Word of God.

I don't have to tell you that Satan looks for any way he can to find entry into your life and home. Here's a brief list of things to look for in your home.

Media

The presence and influence of Satan on the music, videos, television and books that are available today have desensitized most people. Media is not, in and of itself, a problem, but the focus of much of the materials presented today is more darkness than light. Do not be involved with television (via cable or satellite system), films, videos, music or other media that have Satanic, New Age, psychic, horror or occult themes, or that deal with murder, pornography, perversion or inappropriate sexual material. Do not surf the Internet without first filtering information. All games associated with *Wizards of the Coast*, including Pokemon, Dungeons and Dragons and Dragonball Z should be avoided. Other games with high violence ratings that promote anger, rage and murder should be off limits. Scan your bookshelves for books or magazines that deal with any of these areas and get rid of them. They too only give entrance to demonic activity. Other less obvious books may also catch your attention.

Be very sensitive to the Holy Spirit in all of these areas and ask Him to help you monitor what you and your family engage in. Images are power. Be watchful regarding what you allow to enter your eyes and hear with your ears. Satan often uses these gates to our senses to get access into our lives and homes.

Objects

We've all bought things, received gifts, inherited items or acquired souvenirs that have the potential of providing demons a point of entry into our households. Often tribal objects present problems. Check over items from Native American, African, Mayan, Aztec, Filipino and Haitian cultures. Ethnicity is not necessarily the problem although all ethnic groups have their own set of demonic connections stemming from geographic and root spirits. Instead the issue is with the demonic practices of each culture that are transferred to objects including a piece of artwork, jewelry, mask or other object.

All occult, ritual and temple objects must be avoided. If you have them in your home now, they must be broken, burned and totally destroyed. There is no middle ground on these items. God is clear in Deuteronomy 7:25-26 and 12:3, as well as in Acts 19:18-19, regarding idolatrous, ritual, temple and magical items.

Many people pick up souvenir items that at first seem harmless, but carry occult power. When visiting other parts of the world, make sure you hear from the Holy Spirit regarding any item you decide to purchase. Then anoint it, pray over it, break all curses, spells, hexes and demonic assignments before bringing them into your home.

More Than a Souvenir

Not too long ago, before going on a short trip out of town, several friends got together to do some ministry at another friend's house. They were all familiar with deliverance ministry. The young woman had been dealing with some pretty intense ministry cases over the past six months and was under attack.

Once in the house, they all noticed a ceramic dog, colorfully painted—the kind you pick up in border towns. When they asked where she had gotten the dog, the friend said her mother had sent it from a small town in Mexico. They all decided that the object needed to be destroyed, so they began to pray. Then one young man in the group began to break it into pieces, smashing it against the floor. Only one large piece remained, near the head of the dog. With one kick he brought his right foot down on the neck,

> When praying about your heirlooms or antiques, keep a watchful eye for objects that represent other gods, religions, the occult, or secret societies.

sending the pieces flying everywhere. Sensing victory, they finished praying, gathered up their luggage and started for the resort.

After they had been on the road less than 30 minutes, a call came in from the young man who had crushed the dog's head. Pain was shooting through his right foot and moving up his leg. He could hardly depress the gas pedal when he asked them to pull over at the next exit to pray. Everyone piled out of their cars and began to pray. The pain persisted. They continued. As they addressed every hex, spell and curse, the pain left and the young man was fine. Apparently a witch who had recently visited the owner of the house had placed a hex on the object.

Keeping It in the Family

Family heirlooms that have been handed down from generation to generation or antique items purchased privately or via an auction may have familiar spirits from dead relatives or past owners. That's why it is good, when purchasing an item, to ask questions and get as much information as you can on the antique. Pray over it and allow the Holy Spirit to guide your decision regarding the final purchase. Then when you get it home, anoint it, break any curses and allow God to cleanse and bless it.

When praying about your heirlooms or antiques, keep a watchful eye for objects that represent other gods, religions, the occult or secret societies. Scripture is clear about God's hatred for the worship of false gods. Be aware of the telltale signs of hidden idolatry as you look over your heirlooms and antiques. All of these items, as well as those used in temple worship and occult rituals, must be destroyed or have the curses broken. Most of the time they have to be destroyed.

Other Gods

Any object in your house that has a carved, painted or stone image of an idol, god or demonic figure should be removed. More specifically, your home should be free of Buddhas, fertility gods and goddesses, Greek and Roman gods, gargoyles, Native American dreamcatchers, kachinas, totem poles (in most cases), fetishes, and Aztec, Mayan or other idolatrous items from ancient cultures. You should avoid demonic or evil distorted representations of lions, dragons or other creatures.

Anti-Christ Religions

If you or other members of your family have been involved with false religions, keep these things in mind while cleansing your possessions. All materials related to the New Age, Islam, Hinduism, Buddhism, other eastern religions, Christian Science, native religions and all cults including Mormonism, Jehovah's Witnesses, the Moonies, The Way International and others should be removed from your home and burned. By no means is this an exhaustive list of materials that are available in this category, but it provides a starting place for you to do some "house cleaning."

Occult Materials and Objects

All occult materials or objects must be completely destroyed. There are no exceptions. All objects used in rituals, amulets, Ouija boards, tarot cards, crystals, crystal balls, 8 balls, voodoo dolls, fetishes, dreamcatchers, native worship drums, water witching and rain sticks (used in worship), obelisks and any other pagan symbols and statues. Any materials, objects or items connected to satanism, witchcraft, black magic, demon worship, spirit guides, fortune telling, palmistry or practices in the New Age should be destroyed as well.

Break, crush or burn these objects. Do not simply throw them in the trash for someone else to pick up. Remember what Deuteronomy 7:25-26 says: "You shall burn the carved images of their gods with fire; you shall not covet the silver or gold that is on them, nor take it for yourselves, lest you be snared by it; for it is an abomination to the Lord your God. Nor shall you bring an abomination into your house, lest you be doomed to destruction like it. You shall utterly detest it and utterly abhor it, for it is an accursed thing."

Freemasonry and Other Secret Societies

Freemasonry is widespread across the United States and around the world and is often passed down family lines from generation to generation. Its hidden rituals of initiation and occult degrees are totally against God's Word. Whether you or your ancestors have been Masons, Shriners, Knights of Columbus, Knights Templars or members of any other ungodly secret societies, the rings, regalia, books and objects used in the ceremonies must be destroyed.

Recently I heard the story of a woman in another city who met some of my students. They met at church and began talking about their lives. After a little while, family came up in the conversation and the woman mentioned that her grandfather had been a Mason. He had given her some of his ceremonial items. She had them framed and put them on one of the walls in her home. One of the students told her a little about the occult roots of masonry and suggested that she destroy the items. The comment brought a quick and sharp response from the woman who said, "I'll die first before I get rid of those!"

Needless to say, the conversation ended with that. Two weeks later doctors discovered that she had cancer. She called one of the students and told her what had happened. Within several days I met her when I spoke at the church. I prayed for her healing and told her to repent, go home and burn the objects. She did. Within a week her doctors had miraculous news. The cancer was totally gone.

Whatever God puts His finger on in your home, be quick to do what He says regardless of the monetary value or sentimental attachment. Stay away from anything that opens your home to demonic activity, relates to the kingdom of darkness, hints of evil and doesn't give glory to God.

Chapter 4

A Dwelling Place—
Habitation for Glory

The glory—Moses saw it when He encountered Jehovah, the Lord God Almighty on Mt. Sinai. God desired a place of habitation where He could fellowship with His creation. He told Moses, in Exodus 25:8, "Let them make Me a sanctuary; that I may dwell among them." God wanted to restore the intimacy He had with His creation in the Garden. He wanted a place where He could dwell with His people.

It's hard for us today to understand the fullness of the glory of God that the first man and woman knew in the Garden. Sometimes we reach that place when we enter into His presence during prayer and worship. For most though, it isn't a daily experience. Adam and Eve walked in the habitation of God's glory daily. The fullness of His presence wasn't an occasional thing with them. They had unrestricted access. They talked face to face with God and walked with Him in the coolness of the day.

The Tabernacle of God

When that level of intimacy and closeness was lost because of man's

31

rebellion, God looked for another way to "dwell among His people."
Even though God had a habitation in Heaven surrounded by the worship
of angels, He craved companionship, communion and fellowship with
his creation. He missed the intimacy He shared with those that shared
His likeness. He wanted to be one again with His man and woman. He
wanted to walk and talk and reveal Himself to them again.

For the time being, God chose a tent to be His habitation. According
to the laws and ordinances He gave Moses at Mt. Sinai, He agreed to
meet man on his own level and make His habitation a tent. God's
tabernacle would not be a permanent dwelling. It was but a shadow of
the temple that would be promised to David and later built by his son
Solomon. David cried out in
the Psalms, "I will not give
sleep to mine eyes, or
slumber to mine eyelids,
Until I find out a place for
the Lord, an habitation for
the mighty God of Jacob"
(Psalm 132:4-5). Solomon
would fulfill David's
deepest dream and desire.

> Jesus paved the way for
> us to receive the restoration
> of dominion and authority
> in the earth and become
> the habitation for God's
> glorious presence.

First Chronicles 22:6-8 says, "Then he called for Solomon his son, and
charged him to build an house for the Lord God of Israel. And David
said to Solomon, My son, as for me, it was in my mind to build an
house unto the name of the Lord my God: But the word of the Lord
came to me, saying, Thou hast shed blood abundantly, and hast made
great wars; thou shalt not build an house unto my name, because thou
hast shed much blood upon the earth in my sight."

Even though David would amass a great amount of materials for
the temple of God, his son would be the builder. David had unclean
hands. The blood he had shed as a murderer and a man of war
disqualified him before God. The blood of Uriah and those killed in
battle cried out for justice. Just like the blood of Abel had cried out
generations before, their souls demanded restitution. We will examine

this principle of the blood in more detail later in the book.

David would still play a key part in the temple's construction. According to Ruth Specter Lascelle's handbook *Jewish Faith and the New Covenant*, David collected over $87 billion worth of materials for the temple. That's a lot of money, especially before inflation. Gold, silver and brass totaled $34 billion, jewels another $34 billion, vessels of gold and silver over $4 billion, robes and vestments $10 billion, trumpets $1 billion and other rough materials $12 billion. The food bill to feed the workman alone totaled $344 million.

Habitation for Glory

This temple would give a glimpse into the habitation that God would one day establish in the hearts of men, as the temple of His Holy Spirit. After the building was completed, the glory of the Lord came and filled the temple. The shekinah of God's presence dwelt between the cherubim and over the Mercy Seat. God had chosen to dwell in the temple because man, who once lived in tents, now lived in buildings. God's desire was again to communicate with man on his level. Ruth Specter Lacelle writes: "God lived in The Tent while His people were wandering, but in a Temple when His people were settled in the Land."

Living Stones

This building was still not God's final habitation. Sin once again caused God to withdraw His presence from among the people. A better house was coming, one that was made without wood and stone and metals. God wanted to set up residence in man himself as the temple of the living God.

He did with His Son Jesus Christ. Jesus paved the way for us to receive the restoration of dominion and authority in the earth and become the habitation for God's glorious presence. "His body became the dwelling place of the Father! Messiah Jesus was the anti-type of the altars, the tent in the wilderness, and the Temple of Solomon! Between the cherubim over the Mercy Seat of his heart dwelt the Shekinah! He is the true Tabernacle which the Lord pitched and not man. Everything about the Temple and the Tabernacle pointed to the Messiah Yeshua!" writes Lacelle. Once again God had come down to man's level. He had subjected Himself to a body formed out of the dust of the earth. He humbled Himself. He came and dwelt in the flesh of a man so that man could dwell in the glory of God.

One more time man's sin and rebellion would remove God's habitation on the Earth. Jesus became the ultimate sacrifice for man's rebellion. Colossians 1:19-22 says, "For it pleased the Father that in Him all the fullness should dwell, and by Him to reconcile all things to Himself, by Him, whether things on earth or things in heaven, having made peace through the blood of His cross. And you, who once were alienated and enemies in your mind by wicked works, yet now He has reconciled in the body of His flesh through death, to present you holy, and blameless, and above reproach in His sight."

Jesus gave His life to establish a new habitation for God's glory. Now cleansed and made ready for God's glory, man's heart would become a portal for His presence. First Corinthians 3:16 says, "Do you not know that you are the temple of God and that the Spirit of God dwells in you?"

We are God's dwelling place. We are His habitation. He lives in us and we live in Him. "Eye has not seen, nor ear heard, nor have entered into the heart of man the things which God has prepared for those who love Him. But God has revealed them to us through his Spirit. For the Spirit searches all things, yes the deep things of God. For what man knows the things of a man except the spirit of the man which is in him? Even so no one knows the things of God except the Spirit of God. Now we have received, not the spirit of the world, but the Spirit who is from God, that we might know the things that have been freely given to us by God" (1 Corinthians 2:9-12).

Beyond Spring Cleaning

We need to take God's indwelling seriously. He will not dwell in a place where darkness and light abide together. He will not remain in an unclean house. He will remove His presence from a dwelling that has been defiled by sin, rebellion and idolatry.

God is unchanging. What caused Him to remove His presence from the first man and woman in the Garden still causes Him to depart from our lives today. He cannot and will not cleanse your physical property, home and possessions until the dwelling place of your heart is free from defilement. The great lie is that you can live as you want and God will always provide protection. He dwells in purity and holiness. Ask Him to cleanse the temple of your heart today as you pray this prayer:

Lord Jesus, come create in me a clean heart, O God, and renew a right spirit within me. Create a place where You can come and dwell. Restore my heart to purity and holiness. Remove every defilement in my spirit, soul and body that keeps me from loving and serving You completely with my whole heart. Shine the light of Your presence into every dark corner of my life. Help me, God, to be willing to give You every hidden area that would keep me from fellowship and intimacy with You. Take the things that are wrong in my life and make them right so that my heart can be a habitation for Your glory. I acknowledge Jesus Christ as the light of my life and receive His cleansing power. Amen.

Chapter 5

Portals—Entry Into the Supernatural

Portals—it's a popular word these days. *Webster's New Collegiate Dictionary* defines a portal as "a door or gate, an approach or entrance to a bridge or tunnel." New Agers and those in the occult claim that electrical and magnetic gateways provide spiritual portals to parallel dimensions. They believe, like those before them, that there are spiritual doorways waiting to be unlocked. Since pagan times, those who practice "the craft" have recognized energy fields called leylines. Strange mystical powers seem to be tied to these areas, creating prime property for places of worship, burial grounds and sacred high places. Ancient people built their temples, pyramids and altars on these grounds where the Earth's energy was the strongest.

Today's practitioners of the New Age movement recognize the existence of these portals of power. But what they don't know is that these doorways are not to the third heaven, but to the second heaven and the demonic realm in the earth. The false light they are following has delivered a counterfeit instead of the "real thing."

A Supernatual Connection

Ancient legends alone are not the only source of information. Science continues to search for a more conclusive answer. According to *Science News*, the weekly news magazine of science, new theories lean toward a world where "...everything in the universe is composed of tiny loops or strings of energy vibrating in a space-time that has six or seven extra dimensions beyond the seemingly endless three standard dimensions of space and one of time."

Everywhere you turn these days, people are looking for a supernatural connection. Men, women and even children are searching for something that reaches beyond the ordinary. According to a 1999 CNN-Gallop poll, 70 million Americans believe it's possible to communicate with the dead. Ghostwriter Glen Grant says, "One in four Americans claims to have seen a ghost. The belief in an afterlife is extremely high in America—much higher than any other industrial nation." A Honolulu mediator, psychic and counselor, Angelina Joseph, who teaches classes in intuitive development is quoted as saying that "People have a deep need for connections that are more real than real."

That's not new. What is new is that it's so in the mainstream. It's gone Hollywood. In ever increasing numbers, people are calling psychic hotlines for a quick glimpse into their future. Thousands watch as others contact their dead relatives on television. What they probably don't realize is that they have most likely made a connection with demonic spirits and not the dead.

Spirit to Spirit

Look at the list of movies over the past few years: *Interview With A Vampire, The Blair Witch Project, The Sixth Sense, Dracula, End of Days,* and *Lost Souls,* just to mention a few. Even more of the demonic fills the small screen, with the major networks offering up *Buffy the Vampire*

Slayer, Witchblade, and the miniseries *The Mists of Avalon*—a new twist on the old theme of King Arthur and the Knights of the Round Table. Then there's Pokemon, Dragonball Z and the Harry Potter series which zero in on the hearts of younger children. According to Christie Hirata, the lead clerk at Borders Books Music and Café at Ward Center in Honolulu, it's all about "...Everything spiritual, metaphysical, numerological, magical, mystical and astrological."

Everywhere people are seeking something to fill the spiritual vacuum. They are seeking a spirit-to-spirit connection. Man, who is spirit, made in the likeness and image of God, is called to worship God in spirit and in truth. Instead, people all over the world are reaching for another kind of supernatural experience that is leading them into the realm of darkness.

> Everywhere people are seeking something to fill the spiritual vacuum. They are seeking a spirit-to-spirit connection.

A God-shaped Vacuum

In 41 years of ministry, I've seen a lot of people. All of them, in one way or another, have been searching for someone to fill their deepest longing. The only One Who can fill that longing and emotional vacuum is God. He is the One Who first breathed life into them. That's the Spirit-to-spirit connection people are searching for. The very Spirit of God, described in Hebrew as "ruah" or breath and in Greek as "pneuma" or wind, is the supernatural power that makes man like God. God's Spirit hovered over the earth during creation. He gave man life in Genesis 2:7. He is the same Spirit Who takes up residence in the heart of man and creates a portal for God's continuous presence.

People everywhere are looking for that supernatural experience. Many are ending up with counterfeits. Even some Christians are leaving doors open to the enemy of their souls. What doors are people opening? Who or what are they letting into their lives? What connection have they made with the dark side?

Hell on Earth

It was an old house in a remote area of the city. The family had lived in the home for 30 years. In all of that time, nothing unusual had ever happened until late in April. For nine months straight the family of four, including Michael, his wife, Stephanie, and their sons, David and John, experienced hell on Earth. Nightmare on Elm Street had come to their neighborhood. They constantly felt like they were living in the middle of the worst horror movie of all time.

The couple's youngest son, John, was the first to be troubled by the events in the home. He had always been a special child and very sensitive to spiritual things. One day what looked like an elderly woman appeared in his bedroom. The woman looked like one of his great aunts, but was likely a familiar spirit. At first he wasn't frightened, fooled by the appearance of the spirit, but then it lunged toward him several times. It tried to knock him against the wall.

> They constantly felt like they were living in the middle of the worst horror movie of all time.

Hearing the commotion, his mother ran into the room. Like her son, she too could see into the supernatural realm. The spirit, still masquerading as the great aunt, turned, glared at her and said, "I have forsaken her and God will forsake her." Even though the voice was not audible, both the mother and her son heard the exact same statement from within their spirit. To them it was an announcement of more horrific things to come.

In the weeks that followed, the family's dog, Cisco, sustained a strange injury that almost killed him. One of the bathroom toilets gushed water continually and foul smells filled the rooms of the house. Then just weeks before her older son David's confirmation, the family was sitting in the den. A demonic spirit that looked like an ancient medusa with four heads appeared on the ceiling. Surrounded by fire, it hovered for a minute and then settled on the couch between David, Mary and Michael. It remained for quite some time. Soon other demons took up residence in the house, tormenting all of the family members except Michael. Their nightly threat of "We're here to kill you" resulted in an atmosphere of terror.

Desperate for help, the family called a Catholic friend who brought some holy water and candles over to the house. Night after night the entire family huddled in one room. They sprinkled holy water on the bed, lit candles and prayed. Each morning they were thankful that they had made it through another night. They thought they were going to die.

Months passed. Halloween came and went. Their nerves were getting frayed and the fear was increasing. Each night more demons came. Some attacked the boys. Other sexual demons tormented Mary. Michael knew what they had to do. He packed up his family and they left.

Peaceful at Last

Not long after they left and were living in a local motel, a friend gave Michael my business card. He called me and I made an appointment to come out to their house. As I walked through the house, nothing in particular caught my attention until I reached the very center of the land. Once there I knew by a word of knowledge that the land had been dedicated to the enemy. The only way to cleanse and reclaim the land was to stake it and anoint the property.

Together with Michael and the rest of the family, I put a stake in the center of the property and on each of the corners. Then I poured the anointing oil over each stake and we prayed and rededicated the land to the Lord. Peace was finally restored. The bloodline curse that had opened the door to a demonic portal was closed and locked.

Over the years I have discovered five doors that allow Satan and his demonic forces to gain entrance, take up residence and develop strongholds. These are disobedience or willful sin, unforgiveness, inner vows and judgments, trauma and generational curses. I talk extensively about each of these doors and how to close them in my first book, *Shadow Boxing*. I would encourage you, if you haven't already, to find out what doors you or your ancestors have left open.

Highway to Heaven

Satan isn't the only one who uses portals, doors and gates. John Paul Jackson, in a recent teaching, provided this definition of a heavenly portal. It is "a doorway or passageway—a cylinder of light offering divine protection by which angels and heavenly beings can come and go, without demonic interference. Portals from God begin in the third Heaven, travel through the second Heaven, and open upon Earth." Portals exist all around the Earth.

These portals or doorways to God's presence are cited throughout Scripture. Psalm 24:7 says, "Lift up your heads, O you gates! And be lifted up, you everlasting doors! And the King of glory shall come in." Revelation 4:1-2 declares: "After these things I looked, and behold, a door standing open in heaven. And the first voice which I heard was like a trumpet speaking with me, saying 'Come up here, and I will show you things which must take place after this.' Immediately, I was in the Spirit..." God wants us to be expectant regarding His appearing. He desires that we watch for Him.

Doors and gates are often mentioned throughout the Bible as ways that God establishes communication with us. Revelation 3:20 says Jesus stands at the door and declares, "Behold, I stand at the door and knock. If anyone hears My voice and opens the door, I will come in to him and dine with him, and he with Me." It's a door that offers a choice—open your heart to God, or close it.

In the Old Testament, gates were critical points of entry to walled cities. They were heavily fortified. Access was controlled. At night or in times of danger they were closed and guarded. Leaders, elders and other government officials sat at the gates and made their rulings. Contracts were made, business conducted and announcements from God made just outside the gates of the city. Gates were important places.

In the New Testament, John 10:9-10 speaks of Jesus as the gate to the sheep pen: "I am the door. If anyone enters by Me, he will be saved, and will go in and out and find pasture. The thief does not come except to steal, and to kill, and to destroy. I have come that they may have life, and that they may have it more abundantly."

The sheep pen was a yard attached to a dwelling. In that yard was a single gate for the sheep. High stone walls topped with thorn bushes surrounded it. Jesus is the gate. He brings protection, safety and salvation to the sheep. The warning to all believers or "sheep" is to make sure we enter by His gate alone. Then and only then are we free from the intrusive attacks of Satan who

> ## Portals from God begin in the third Heaven, travel through the second Heaven, and open upon Earth.

comes as a thief to steal, kill and destroy.

Jesus speaks of gates again in Matthew 7:13-14: "Enter by the narrow gate; for wide is the gate and broad is the way that leads to destruction, and there are many who go in by it. Because narrow is the gate and difficult is the way which leads to life, and there are few who find it." Many people, even Christians today, seek a path of their own choosing. But Jesus says the path of life is narrow. It is a portal to God's presence which is strictly controlled and where access is granted only to those who choose to walk the path to life eternal.

Restricted Access

Jesus declares that those who choose to walk as close to God as possible will achieve victory over "the gates of Hades." The Greek word used in Matthew 16:18 is katischyo. It means to "overcome" or "be stronger than." When we control access in our lives to God alone and provide a portal for His presence, the forces of hell cannot win. We become overcomers. We are conquerors. We are victorious. Paul says in Romans 8:37, "We are more than conquerors through Him Who loved us."

God fights our battles and He always win. As we continue to examine the portals to cleansing throughout this book, I want you to remember that "The battle is the Lord's" (1 Samuel 17:47). "Some trust in chariots, and some in horses; But we will remember the name of the Lord our God" (Psalm 20:7). "The horse is prepared for the day of battle, But deliverance is of the Lord." (Proverbs 21:31) Allow God to come with His mighty, delivering presence and remove every curse on your life, land and possessions.

Part Two

Generation After Generation

Chapter 6

Curses—Truth
and Consequences

Recently someone was telling about an episode of *Friday the 13th-The Series*. They had stayed up late one night and just happened to see a story called "The Maestro." Not accustomed to watching horror shows, they started to change the channel. They watched for a minute.

The story chronicled the life of a crippled choreographer. Only the most talented dancers were allowed to study with him. He would instruct each one regarding the aspects of dance. He would perfect their technique. Then when he knew he had captured their heart, he commanded them to swear an oath on an antique music box. Once they had pledged to give their soul and body to the dance, even to the death, the music box was opened and notes began to play. The music became frantic. The dancer struggled. The choreographer taunted. As the story continued, it became clear that the music box was cursed, and the notes played a deadly song that drove each of the dancers to their death.

The story left a lasting impression. Curses do exist. They affect people's lives and they carry real and lasting consequences from generation to generation.

The Reality of Curses

The word curse is used 230 times in Scripture. I've always believed that if God says it once, it's important. If He says it two or three times, it's *very* important. So think how *extremely important* it must be if He mentions something 230 times. God wants to get our attention about the reality of curses. He wants us to know what they are and how they can affect our lives. A curse is the exact opposite of a blessing. It is the calling down of evil on someone or something. It is the inflicting of a judgment.

Challenging Authority

When Satan was handed the authority of the earth from Adam and Eve through their disobedience, God had no other choice but to pronounce curses on all involved. He had placed Adam and Eve in the Garden and told them that only one thing would bring a curse of death on their lives. In Genesis 2:17 God made them a promise. He let them know, in no uncertain terms, that if they ate of the tree of the knowledge of good and evil, they would suffer the curse of death. Not only would they die physically, but spiritually as well.

Satan knew when he challenged the authority of the man and woman that he was attacking all that God had said to them. He wanted them to believe his lie, forget the truth and break their covenant with God. He knew that if he could get them to violate their covenant, they would lose control of the earth and all God's blessings. Satan understood the character of God. He realized that God would never back away from the covenant He had made. He was certain that no matter how much it hurt, God would enforce the curse and remove the blessing. Now that Adam and Eve had both eaten of the fruit, they would reap the consequences of their actions.

Curses and Consequences

The truth had its blessings, but disobedience had its curses and consequences. Genesis 3:14-19 lists the curses that came on all that had been a part of this act of treason. The serpent was the first to be cursed. Verse 14 of Chapter 3 says, "Because you have done this, you are cursed more than all cattle, and more than every beast of the field. On your belly you shall go and you shall eat dust all the days of your life." The serpent that once walked upright would lose his legs and be the most cursed among all the animals. He would slither along the ground on his belly and eat dust.

The curse was not just on the serpent, but on the "old serpent" Satan himself. His part in leading the snake to be his accomplice would lead to his eventual destruction when Jesus Christ would crush his head. The last part of Genesis 3:15 says, "...He (Jesus) shall bruise (or crush) your head, and you shall bruise His heel." Genesis 3:15 adds, "And I will put enmity Between you and the woman, And between your seed and her Seed." Satan and the woman would be at odds. There would always be conflict between them because a woman would eventually give birth to the Messiah, the Anointed One and the Deliverer. Mary, the mother of

> Satan knew that if he could get them to violate their covenant, they would lose control of the earth and all God's blessings.

Jesus, would give birth to the One Who would finally insure Satan's defeat. The great dragon of Revelation 12:9 who "...was cast out, that serpent of old, called the Devil and Satan, who deceives the whole world; he was cast to the earth, and his angels were cast out with him," would at the end of the age be "...cast into the lake of fire and brimstone where the beast and the false prophet are. And they will be tormented day and night forever and ever" (Revelation 20:10).

The woman was next to receive judgment. Her curse would involve sorrow in conception, pain in childbirth and a new position of subservience. Before the Fall, she stood with Adam on an equal footing. They were co-rulers of the earth. Together they shared dominion and authority as a gift from God. But now, as a consequence for her rebellion, she would no longer be equal in authority. She would take a role under Adam. She would serve him. She would be at all times, subject to his authority. Genesis 3:16 says, "I will greatly multiply your sorrow and your conception; in pain you shall bring forth children; your desire shall be for your husband. And he shall rule over you." It would take the blood of Jesus to restore the woman to her former position of authority and equality.

Adam's sin brought a curse of death on his life. Genesis 3:17 says, "Because you have heeded the voice of your wife, and have eaten from the tree of which I commanded you, saying, 'You shall not eat of it.'" Adam would get no reprieve from God even though he was the second to eat of the fruit. He stood next to Eve during her conversation with the serpent. He had the same authority as Eve. He could have stepped in and tried to stop her. But more than that, once she had eaten, he could have chosen God over her and refused to take the bite. His disobedience cost him his life, and would make the rest of his days difficult.

Prior to his rebellion, Adam had labored in the Garden of God without stress, sweat and toil. All that his hand touched succeeded and the land which now would receive its own curse, had formerly yielded maximum harvest. It wouldn't be an easy life anymore. Adam would face a lifetime of work with no early retirement. Verse 19 of Chapter 3 adds, "In the sweat of your face you shall eat bread till you return to the ground. For out of it you were taken; for dust you are and to dust you shall return."

Four More Judgments

God handed down four other judgments. The land would be filled with thistles and thorns and never again yield a maximum harvest. Genesis 3:17-18 declares, "Cursed is the ground for your sake; in toil you shall eat of it, all the days of your life. Both thorns and thistles it shall bring forth for you, and you shall eat the herb of the field." Even the earth would reap the consequences of Adam and Eve's rebellion. The land was now open to the devastating effects of sin and judgment. We still see that judgment today all around the world.

The animal kingdom was also judged. In Genesis 2:19-20: "Out of the ground the Lord God formed every beast of the field and every bird of the air, and brought them to Adam to see what he would call them. And whatever Adam called each living creature that was its name. So Adam gave names to all cattle, to the birds of the air, and to every beast of the field." Prior to the entrance of sin in the earth, even the animals experienced peace. They dwelt together without conflict. There was no fear between one species and another. The food chain of the animal kingdom which would later afflict the beasts of the field, didn't exist.

Romans 8:20-22 gives insight into just how much the animal kingdom was affected by Adam and Eve's disobedience: "For the creation was subjected to futility, not willingly, but because of Him who subjected it in hope; because the creation itself also will be delivered from the bondage of corruption into the glorious liberty of the children of God. For we know that the whole creation groans and labors with birth pangs together until now." The birds of the air, the beasts of the field and all of the animal kingdom is waiting for the moment in time when the sons of God are manifest in the earth and balance restored.

One more judgment remained. God had to enforce man's breach of His covenant. Romans 6:23 says, "For the wages of sin is death, but the gift of God is eternal life in Christ Jesus our Lord." Because of their choice to serve Satan, the man and the woman, and all those born later, would face the curse of physical, spiritual and eternal death. God's plan to remove the curse from man would cost Him His Son and would take generations.

The fourth judgment sent man from the Garden. Genesis 3:22-24 reads, "Then the Lord God said, 'Behold, the man has become like one of Us, to know good and evil. And now, lest he put out his hand and take also of the tree of life, and eat, and live forever'—therefore the Lord God sent him out of the garden of Eden to till the ground from which he was taken. So He drove out the man; and He placed cherubim at the east of the garden of Eden, and a flaming sword which turned every way, to guard the way to the tree of life."

God moved quickly to prevent His creation from making another mistake. If they ate of the tree of life, they would both live forever in a state of sin. They would be Satan's captives. God would have no way to redeem their lives and save them from eternal destruction. He would have to do the one thing that would break His heart—drive them out of the Garden. Before He did that, God would shed the blood of animals to cover their sin.

A Covenant of Blood

Adam and Eve had been clothed with the glorious presence of God. When they sinned, they fashioned fig-leaf garments to cover their nakedness, guilt and shame. They tried to make themselves more acceptable to God. Their breaking of the covenant God had made with them in the Garden required death. It was the ultimate sentence for their actions.

God Himself carried out the sentence and shed the first blood. He took an innocent animal, killed it, and clothed them with its skin and fur. By doing so, God set in motion a pattern of substitution. It would be a part of every one of His covenants until Jesus would be the final sacrifice for all men.

Before Jesus would become that perfect sacrifice of Hebrews 9:12-14, God would make many other covenants with man. After the flood, God made a pact with Noah and sealed it with a rainbow. With Abraham, He cut another covenant that brought the promise of the Messiah. Four hundred and thirty years later, God encountered Moses and made another covenant with His chosen nation Israel. Following the 40 years of wandering in the wilderness, God again made another covenant outlining the conditions for living in the land of promise. When David took the throne of Israel after the death of Saul, God made a pact of kingship. Just before Jesus died in Jerusalem, He made a covenant with the 12 and all those who would believe through His Word and their testimony.

That covenant was the new covenant of His blood. It was an everlasting and eternal covenant. It was the complete fulfillment of every other covenant of God. Jesus' blood would replace all other blood. Hebrews 9:11-15 declares, "But Christ came as High Priest of the good things to come, with the greater and more perfect tabernacle, not made with hands, that is, not of this creation. Not with the blood of goats and calves, but with His own blood He entered the Most Holy Place once for all: having obtained eternal redemption. For if the blood of bulls and goats and the ashes of a heifer, sprinkling the unclean, sanctifies for the purifying of the flesh, how much more shall the blood of Christ, who through the eternal Spirit offered Himself without spot to God, purge your conscience from dead works to serve the living God."

> That covenant was the new covenant of Jesus' blood. It was the complete fulfillment of every other covenant of God.

The body and blood of Jesus would be the one thing every believer could stand on for redemption, cleansing, healing and deliverance. The blood and body of Jesus and the power of His Name would give every child of God authority over all the power of the enemy. Even though Satan was carrying the lease on the Earth, a new lease would be written in blood. It would be unbreakable. It would be irrevocable.

From Generation to Generation

For now the curse would remain in operation and continue from generation to generation. It would be evidenced in many different ways. Not many years ago, a young Chinese missionary contacted me about an object she had in her home that was causing her difficulty. She had received an old rocking chair from her grandfather. Not knowing much about him or the craftsman who made the chair, she thought nothing about having the heirloom in her home.

Not long after receiving it, she sat in the chair. Suddenly she experienced a strange feeling that only got worse over time. Rocking back and forth she felt violated. She sensed someone touching her inappropriately. She felt as if an unseen force, most probably a demon, had sexually molested her.

Over the years I've interviewed and ministered to many women and men who had an incubus or succubus spirit. This type of demonic spirit attacks a person sexually without their permission and develops a strong connection physically, emotionally and spiritually that can sometimes be hard to get rid of. In her case the familiar or demonic spirit had, in my opinion, transferred from her grandfather to his favorite chair and on to her as she sat rocking in the chair. Unable to break the curse attached to the chair, we broke the rocker into pieces and put it in the fireplace to be burned. The fire burned so hot that it blew out the glass doors in front of the fireplace.

But not every heirloom needs to be tossed into the fire. Antiques also are considered in this category and are simply someone else's discarded heirlooms. When you are considering buying an item, look the item over carefully. Check for unfamiliar writing, signs, crests, or objects carved, attached or painted on the piece. Dragons, griffins, double-headed phoenixes or eagles, gargoyles, and snakes often have occult or idolatrous significance and should be avoided, along with Buddhas and other non-Christian religious figures. Any object you don't have peace about shouldn't be purchased and brought into your home.

A Few Antiques

Not long ago, one of my friends was visiting a family in another state. Rather than get a hotel, they offered him their guestroom during his stay. They had acquired a few new antiques since he last visited and wanted him to look them over. They didn't want any demonic spirits hanging around. The home was very peaceful.

One evening they walked through the house room by room. Finally he came upon several items. The first two were matching tables. They had a goddess type figure on the base supports. The third a painting with an ancient Greco-Roman background had a somewhat distorted lion in it. He had a check in his spirit.

Again, not sensing from the Holy Spirit that the items needed to be destroyed, he prayed, broke any curses on the objects and anointed them with oil and blessed them. Not every object needs to be thrown away or destroyed. But all idolatrous, ritual, temple or occult items must be broken, burned and totally destroyed. I'll be telling you more about identifying specific problems with objects in later chapters.

Chapter 7

Cries From the Earth

Dead men do tell tales. Ask any forensic scientist and they will tell you that blood, dirt smudges, scratches, hair fibers, bullet casings and other crime scene evidence can tell you more about what happened at a crime scene than most witnesses. Take, for example, the 30-year-old murder case involving former Green Beret surgeon, Dr. Jeffrey MacDonald.

Even though MacDonald still remains incarcerated in a federal penitentiary for the murder of his wife and two daughters, questions still surround the case. A new book, *Fatal Justice: Reinvestigating the MacDonald Murders*, calls for a new test of the crime scene blood samples. Proponents of MacDonald's innocence are counting on the blood crying out on his behalf. The blood is on the line and MacDonald's freedom hangs in the balance.

I'm not here to debate the guilt or innocence of this man or to argue the evidence of the case. I'll leave that to the lawyers and the scientists. What I do know is that blood cries out for vengeance. It did in Abel's time, and it still does today.

Curses on the Land

The stories are numerous. History records a wide range of "curses" attached to the land. Pick any area of the country or, for that matter, the world and you'll find them. Joyce Dixon, author of the *Southern States Forum,* records this story on her Internet Web site, *Southern Ghosts and Haunted Places.* She tells of a well at Mark's Mill near Warren, Arkansas.

During the Civil War, the Union army threw their comrades' lifeless bodies into the well to cover heavy losses. Witnesses say their moans can be heard coming up from the well below. In another account, Dixon records the tale of a group of African Ibo tribesmen. They were unloaded at Dunbar Creek on St. Simon's Island in Georgia. Instead of facing life as slaves, they turned as a group and marched into the water and drowned. Some say they hear their chanting at the water's edge to this day.

Santa Cruz's News and Issues Web site is full of stories about the California town. One story is connected to an old bone yard—one of three graveyards still in the city. Townspeople say they've come across some pretty angry spirits. The most cursed of the burial ground lies in the Portrero district just off River Street and stretches from the Evergreen Cemetery all to way to Costco. Their locals tell of a young Native American man who was put to death for questioning the authority of his elders. With his last breath, the warrior cursed the tribe and declared that he would haunt the land.

The Blood Cries Out

Mother Chapar, an old Spanish woman and still a resident of Santa Cruz, experienced the curse. She remembers a savage attack. A group of fierce Yachicumne Indians from Stockton invaded Santa Cruz on the very spot. They murdered the local Ohlones. She recalls walking from Portrero to Mission Hill. Her feet never touched the ground because so many bones covered the earth.

Since that slaughter, more than 20 people have lost their lives by accident or violence in the same area. In all of these cases, the "ghostly" apparitions were most likely demonic spirits. They inhabited the spiritual atmosphere because blood had been shed. They allowed the curse to remain. Just as in the time of Cain, the land had been marked with the blood of murder and cried out for justice. The life force of Abel was in his blood. God Who had given Abel life could hear his cries from the blood soaked ground. Job 16:18 declares, "O Earth, do

> ## Just as in the time of Cain, the land had been marked with the blood of murder and cried out for justice.

not cover my blood, and let my cry have no resting place!" Bloodshed that has not been avenged cries out to God for justice. Isaiah 26:21 says, "For behold, the Lord comes out of His place To punish the inhabitants of the earth for their iniquity; the earth will also disclose her blood, And will no more cover her slain." It is impossible for the blood to remain silent or for God to allow iniquity to go unpunished.

The Curse of Cain

Cain's heinous and bloodthirsty murder of Abel brought severe judgment to him and to the land. First God cursed him. Cain's judgment is recorded in Genesis 4:11: "Now you are cursed from the earth, which has opened its mouth to receive your brother's blood from your hand."

Next, God added a second judgment involving both Cain and the land. Scripture says in verse 12, "When you till the ground it shall no longer yield its strength to you...." Interestingly enough Cain's curse was similar to that of his parents Adam and Eve when their disobedience forced God to bring judgment on the land. As with any generational curse, history was repeating itself. Genesis 2:18 says the first curse on the land resulted in "...thorns and thistles."

In Genesis 4:12 the ground would resist man's efforts again. This time, weeds would be the least of Cain's problems. The land would rob him of the fruits of his labor. He would work hard just like his father, but his harvests would always be less than expected. He would never experience a maximum yield. The land had become twice cursed.

The Blame Game

The curse on Cain and the land was just the beginning. God would mark him and send him to a place east of Eden. Genesis 4:12 says: "...A fugitive and a vagabond you shall be on the earth." God's decision greatly disturbed Cain. God had said nothing about the danger Cain might encounter after he left Eden, yet that was all he could think about. The murderer was afraid he would be someone else's target.

Verse 13 reflects his panic and complaint to the Lord. "My punishment is greater than I can bear!"

The man who had no compassion for his brother and didn't want any part of being his keeper, wanted God to be

> Cain must have learned the "blame game" from his parents who had done some "finger pointing" of their own earlier in their lives.

his. He pleaded with the Lord for a reprieve. "Surely You have driven me out this day from the face of the ground; I shall be hidden from Your face; I shall be a fugitive and a vagabond on the earth, and it will happen that anyone who finds me will kill me" (verse 14). Unable to take responsibility for his actions, Cain blamed God for his situation. He must have learned this "blame game" from his parents who had done some "finger pointing" of their own earlier in their lives.

As far as Cain was concerned, things were now getting a little bit out of hand. After all, what was going to happen to him? Someone might do to him what he had done to his brother. He didn't want to be someone's victim. His torment had started.

Greater and Greater Violence

God in His mercy extended grace to Cain. Verse 15 says, "And the

Lord said to him, 'Therefore whoever kills Cain, vengeance shall be taken on him sevenfold.' And the Lord set a mark on Cain, lest anyone finding him should kill him." God, even in judgment, protected Cain. But Cain's iniquity would follow him and multiply as he left God's presence. He would travel, build cities and develop the art and craft of fashioning metals. He would also contribute to the escalating sin that filled the earth.

Cain's bloodline would breed another murderer, Lamech. Genesis 4:23-24 says, "Then Lamech said to his wives: 'Adah and Zillah, hear my voice; Wives of Lamech, listen to my speech! For I have killed a man for wounding me, Even a young man for hurting me. If Cain shall be avenged sevenfold, then Lamech seventy-sevenfold.'"

The earth was filling with greater and greater violence. Then God appointed a man to take the place of Abel. God avenged Abel not only with the judgment of Cain, but with the birth of Seth to Adam and Eve. At 130 years of age, Adam was given a son in his own likeness and after his image. This son, Seth, would call on the name of the Lord, and Adam would trace his lineage through him and his son Enosh.

The torment of the earth was not over. Genesis 6:5-7 says, "Then the Lord saw that the wickedness of man was great in the earth and that every intent of the thoughts of his heart was only evil continually. And the Lord was sorry that He had made man on the earth, and He was grieved in His heart. So the Lord said, 'I will destroy man whom I have created from the face of the earth, both man and beast, creeping thing and birds of the air, for I am sorry that I have made them." Verse 11 says the earth "was corrupt before God, and the Earth was filled with violence."

The blood still cried out. This time, the earth's judgment would be total destruction. God's hope for a new world rested with Noah and his family. He would put the earth into the hands of a man one more time.

Avenging the Innocent

From Noah's day until now, the earth has witnessed the shedding of innocent blood. Broken covenants, slaughters, wars, murders, the

Holocaust, genocide, infanticide and worldwide abortion in unprecedented numbers, has left millions of souls without justice. God will not stand by and be mocked. These lives will be avenged. Justice will come for the souls of men, women and the unborn. But vengeance belongs to the Lord alone. Violence is again filling the earth.

Jesus Himself warned that the coming of the Son of Man would be like the days of Noah. Matthew 24:37-39 says, "But as the days of Noah were, so also will the coming of the Son of Man be. For as in the days before the flood, they were

> God will not stand by and be mocked. But vengeance belongs to the Lord alone.

eating and drinking, marrying and giving in marriage, until the day that Noah entered the ark, and did not know until the flood came and took them all away, so also will the coming of the Son of Man be."

Man's iniquity will again cause God to destroy the Earth one more time. We are not far from the same level of iniquity that brought God's judgment in Noah's day. What I am talking about is more than one sin. It's a pattern of iniquity. It is a bentness or propensity toward something. It is a system of behavior or way of life. Cain's murder of Abel brought a generational iniquity to his descendants and a curse on the Earth. His murderous anger, indifference, unrepentant attitude and refusal to see things God's way produced a bloodline that was bent away from God, not toward Him.

It is not only the Old Testament that teaches God's swift action to avenge the shedding of innocent blood, but the New Testament as well. Jesus gives a stern warning in Matthew 23:29-36. His language against the religious leaders of His day, the Pharisees, is unusually strong. His indictment starts in verse 27: "Woe to you, scribes and Pharisee, hypocrites! For you are like whitewashed tombs which indeed appear beautiful outwardly, but inside are full of dead men's bones and all uncleanness." Tombs were whitewashed during this time so that people would not touch them. If they did they would become ceremonially defiled.

Jesus continues in verses 33-35, "Serpents, brood of vipers! How can you escape the condemnation of hell? Therefore, indeed, I send you prophets, wise men, and scribes: some of them you will kill and crucify, and some of them you will scourge in your synagogues and persecute from city to city, that on you may come all the righteous blood shed on the earth, from the blood of righteous Abel to the blood of Zechariah, son of Berechiah, whom you murdered between the temple and the altar." Jesus was exposing the murderous spirit in their hearts. He wanted them to know that judgment was coming. They would not escape God's vengeance against the shedding of innocent blood—not only the blood of Jesus, but of all the other righteous men that had gone before Him. The blood cried out for justice down through the generations. Almighty God would see to it that the scales were balanced in their favor. The guilty would be punished and judgment would be executed.

John, in his Revelation, speaks of a time to come, when the blood of men and women martyred during the Great Tribulation will cry out to God. Revelation 6:10 says, "And they cried with a loud voice, saying, 'How long, O Lord, holy and true, until You judge and avenge our blood on those who dwell on the earth?'" God's answer to all that sacrificed their lives for His truth was recorded in the next verse: "Then a white robe was given to each of them; and it was said to them that they should rest a little while longer, until both the number of their fellow servants and their brethren, who would be killed as they were, was completed." God would not allow their cries to leave His ears. Their innocent blood would be avenged. He still hears the cries of innocents today.

A Dark Foreshadowing

It was a hot, summer day. Out in the middle of nowhere the team working on the case was trying to find the home they were scheduled to cleanse. Along the way they made a wrong turn and ended up in the downtown of a small, rural town in the Midwest. It had an eerie feeling, the kind that causes the hair to stand up on the back of your neck.

There was a sense of darkness and witchcraft. They both wondered if it was a foreshadowing of what they would encounter later. They turned around and headed back, finally finding the home and meeting up with another member of the team.

The ministry had been contacted because Joey, one of the family's young sons, was having nightmares. The child was very sensitive to spiritual things and had been seeing demons in the night. After talking for a few minutes, the team proceeded through the house. Once they arrived in the boy's room, all three of the team sensed something very dark, almost sinister. It was concentrated in one corner of the bedroom.

> They broke the Native American curses and assignments and asked God to remove the demonic guard and close the portal.

Pulling the furniture away to get a better look, they discovered nothing tangible, but felt the presence of a demonic portal or entry point for supernatural activity. They anointed the area with oil and then went outside to the corner of the house and anointed the foundation, bricks and the walls on either side. Then they went to the attic area and prayed over the corners of the home, getting as close to corner of the portal as possible. As they prayed, the peace came and the release to move on. They took the anointing oil and began to pray and pour it along the property lines of the house.

At four different points they stopped and broke curses and assignments. Then they all stopped at a portable metal shed near the corner of the fence line. They all agreed it was another portal. One of the team heard the Spirit of the Lord say, "buffalo hide." They also felt the presence of a demonic guard or sentry posted at one corner of the portal. The team poured the oil around the shed and around the blocks that supported the structure. They broke the Native American curses and assignments and asked God to remove the demonic guard and close the portal.

The release came. They walked the area again and, as before, all three felt peace.

They continued pouring oil around the property and then placed a stake at each corner of the property and blessed it. They got in the car and went to some acreage the family owned on the other side of town.

The land was vacant. As the team walked the property moving across the land three abreast they each saw and felt different things. By the Spirit, one of the team saw a bare tree full of twisted branches and a woman hanging from it. He prayed, broke the curse and moved on. On the other side another member of the team found some animal bones, but felt that they should be buried. She buried them and moved on.

The final member of the team was praying in tongues. It wasn't his usual tongue and he sensed the presence of bloodshed on the land. Then an interpretation came. The land had been used as a hunting ground for local Indians who had inhabited the area. Nothing was found on the remainder of the land. It was cleansed and blessed.

The team returned to the house and prayed over the entire family. From that moment on, the son no longer experienced any difficulty and the peace of the household was restored. The shedding of sacrificial blood by native tribes cried out for vengeance. It was a cry that had held one member of the family captive.

The Perfect Sacrifice

Begin to ask the Holy Spirit to reveal to you the blood that cries out from the sins of your ancestors. Be open to hear from God regarding what you need to do to allow the blood of innocents to be avenged. The blood of Jesus is the perfect sacrifice. His blood is sufficient to cleanse the stained ground of your ancestors that has come down from generation to generation. All God needs is your willingness to hear His voice and obey.

Lord Jesus, please forgive me and my ancestors for their sins in the shedding of innocent blood. I repent of my anger, rage, wrath and murder that have come down through my bloodline and still affects me and my family today. Break off me all my unforgiveness and offenses from my life. Help me to release anything that would lead me to seek revenge against another person or to want evil to come to them. Cleanse my heart, Lord Jesus, of every darkness. Remove every stronghold of generational iniquity and bent toward evil. Today I choose to walk in Your light. May the thoughts and the intents of my heart be toward You continually, and not to evil. I accept Jesus' shed blood to atone for the shedding of innocent blood by me and my ancestors. Amen.

Chapter 8

Paradigm of Pollution

t is the third planet from the sun and has a diameter of over 7900 miles. Once a year it orbits the sun at a distance of 93 million miles. Made up of mostly nitrogen and oxygen it appears from space as a blue and white orb. Its oceans, white clouds and large supply of water may be the reason that it is the only known planet in its solar system to support life. It is Earth.

When God created Earth, He intended it to be a place of dominion for His creation. His desire was for His man and woman to rule the world and enjoy its abundant blessings. For six days God meticulously attended to every detail of His new world. There was light and darkness, day and night. He controlled the atmosphere so that the climate would be comfortable and conducive for life. He added the seas and the dry land. He put grass and herbs and seed on Earth. Stars and planets filled the heavens. He created fish and birds and every kind of living creature. Beasts of every kind and cattle and creeping things filled its landscape. It was all good. There was no death, sickness or disharmony. There was no disaster or calamity. There was complete balance and harmony. Everything was peaceful. It was perfect when man entered the scene.

Rulers of the Earth

Man was God's crowning glory. Adam and Eve were to have been co-rulers of all that God had placed before them. They could have taken the dominion and authority God gave to them as a gift and ruled in righteousness. They could have built a world where every inhabitant would give praise, honor and glory to God. They could have done all of that and more. That was God's desire for His creation.

God had placed the destiny of the earth into Adam and Eve's hands. But in one brief moment, the rule of the earth switched hands. Rebellion had catapulted them from out of God's perfect world into Satan's perverted one. The earth was polluted with the effects of sin. Corruption entered the scene. All the systems of the earth were disrupted. From the stars to the water, from the plants to the animals, everything now shifted from perfection to destruction. The wages of sin had taken root in the earth.

> Pollution began the moment that sin entered the picture. Man's rebellion started the clock ticking on the Earth's destruction.

An Old Problem

Pollution isn't a new thing. It's a very old thing. Today, everyone from New Age prophets, to scientists and activists talk about mass extinction, earthquakes, volcanic eruptions, and a cataclysmic chain of events that will eventually destroy the earth. It's all in the Bible. God foretold it. Pollution started the moment that sin entered the picture. Death came to man when he willfully chose to disobey God. His rebellion started the clock ticking on the earth's destruction. The gross wickedness and violence that filled the world of Noah's day caused God to wipe it out in a flood.

Today the meltdown of the earth continues. According to an "Earth Prophecy" Web site article, *Climate Change and Environmental*

Degradation, the "environment is going to be the main 'national security issue' of the next century." The article lists the issues of global warming, flooding, heat waves and droughts, cold snaps, storms, falling global food production, and growing water scarcity. Missing are the daily reports from other sources of plagues and vaccine resistant diseases. The escalating depletion of resources, the rise of super viruses and the growing world population will not be the thing that eventually destroys the earth. It will be the steadily increasing pollution of man's spiritual, not natural, condition that will lead to his ultimate destruction. That will open the door to the horrors that will come on the earth. It will be pollution like the world has never seen before.

Truth or Lies?

Paul, in his letter to the Church at Rome, describes a gradual progression of twisted spiritual thinking that causes man to exchange the truth of God for a lie. Paul starts by declaring that he is unashamed of the gospel of Jesus Christ in Romans 1:16: "For I am not ashamed of the gospel of Christ, for it is the power of God to salvation for everyone who believes, for the Jew first and also for the Greek." Then he gives a stern warning in verses 18-19: "For the wrath of God is revealed from heaven against all ungodliness and unrighteousness of men, who suppress the truth in unrighteousness, because what may be known of God is manifest in them, for God has shown it to them."

Paul wants his readers to understand that the righteousness he is talking about isn't a "situational ethics" kind of thing. It doesn't differ from situation to situation or person to person. It is determined by God's standard alone. It is not a natural standard, but a divine one. Most of what man is trying to do today is change the world around him by natural means, not spiritual. The word for "wrath" here is God's personal anger. God hates sin. If you don't think so, just go back and read the first 12 chapters of this book or Genesis 1-7. God has always loved man, but has hated his sin. His attitude toward sin will never change.

God's of Our Making

That's why verses 21-31 are so important. Now having built a solid foundation, Paul is going to tell his readers exactly what sin is. He's also going to expose a system of thinking that we'd call today "secular humanism." It's a philosophy that says, "Don't worry, there's no God. There's only man. You're the god. Not god with a little 'g' but 'the GOD' with a big 'G.' It's your life. You're in control." Paul calls that kind of thinking the work of "fools." In verses 22-23 he says, "Professing to be wise, they became fools, and changed the glory of the incorruptible God into an image made like corruptible man—and birds and four-footed animals and creeping things."

The word "fools" is translated from the Greek as "moraino." It means to be a simpleton and a fool. The scripture says those who exchanged the truth of the Word of God for a lie are nothing more than morons. Paul says the worship of God wasn't enough for these simple-headed people. They needed something else—creatures. As you'll find out later in this book, when we talk about altars and graven images, man's exchange of the truth of God for a lie is the root of idolatry. First, man worshiped creeping things, then four-footed beasts, moving on to animals, ending with exaltation of himself.

Everything is downhill from there. Man's heart becomes more and more dark. His thinking is polluted. Perversity and twisted thinking warps the way he looks at life. Not only does it affect his thoughts, but also it produces actions that lead to a pattern of iniquity. That kind of lifestyle moves man farther and farther away from God, and closer and closer to Satan.

Having It Our Way

The seducing spirit of the world has caused man to exchange God's truth for a lie. When he believed the lie, things started to change. Verse 24 says God "gave them up to uncleanness, in the lusts of their hearts...." God let them have their way. God will let you have your way! He didn't create you or anyone else as some kind of robot. He created you with a will of your own and He will let you exercise it. Remember the Frank Sinatra hit *My Way?* God will let you have it "your way." But you'll get the consequences that go with it.

> God will let you have your way. He created you with a will of your own and He will let you exercise it.

Look at verses 25-31. Man exchanged the truth for a lie. He allowed his natural sexual desires to change. He refused to pursue the knowledge of God. So because of that, his mind changed. When his mind changed he opened himself up to "unrighteousness, sexual immorality, wickedness, covetousness, maliciousness" (verse 29). He became "full of envy, murder, strife, deceit, evil-mindedness" (verse 29). Man became "whisperers, backbiters, haters of God, violent, proud, boasters, inventors of evil things, disobedient to parents, undiscerning, untrustworthy, unloving, unforgiving, unmerciful" (verses 29-31). That's quite a list. It sounds a lot like our world today.

Living on the Edge

The paradigm of pollution only leads to more pollution. A little bit of evil never stays a little bit. Paul concludes his teaching in Romans 1:32, "Who, knowing the righteous judgment of God, that those who practice such things are deserving of death, not only do the same but also approve of those who practice them." Not only did these men and women continue to rebel against God and do every kind of evil that was in their dark hearts, they approved of others who wanted to do the same. They had decided to run with a crowd that wouldn't question their lifestyle. They sought out relationships that supported their compromises. Deliverance wasn't on their agenda.

I find that many Christians today think they can play both sides against the middle. They like to get as close to the world as they can and not slip over into hell. I'd rather get so close to God that I might get translated into His presence, than get that close to Satan. Romans

12:1-2, *The Phillips Translation* says, "With eyes wide open to the mercies of God, I beg you my brothers, as an act of intelligent worship, to give Him your bodies, as a living sacrifice, consecrated to Him and acceptable by Him. Don't let the world around you squeeze you into its own mold, but let God re-make you so that your whole attitude of mind is changed. Thus you will prove in practice that the will of God is good, acceptable to Him and perfect."

God wants each of us to develop an attitude of thinking and a consistent lifestyle that communicate His power and His presence to others. People shouldn't be looking at our lives and wondering whether we believe in God or not. Instead, they should be so captivated by what they see that they will want what we have. As the world around us becomes darker, I pray that all believers will become bright, shining lights that let everyone know that we have been "translated from darkness into the light of Jesus Christ."

Take a moment and ask God to show you areas where your thinking and behavior have changed and moved farther away from His Word. Allow Him to put His finger on lies that you have believed about Him. Let Him show you where Satan has squeezed you into the world's way of doing things. Let the Holy Spirit remove all the "spiritual pollution" in your heart, life and home.

Chapter 9

Deadly Obsessions

All that glitters isn't gold. It's true. Ask the tourist that has gotten a "real deal" on a Rolex on the streets of a major U.S. city or foreign country. The vendor talked a good game. After all it looked like the famous name brand. At least it did to the casual observer. To the seasoned jeweler it isn't hard to see it for what it really is—a blatant fake. The representation of the real just doesn't stack up to the real thing.

Mankind has always been easily deceived by the shiny outward appearance of things. Beginning in the Garden, man found it difficult and way too tempting to look past the appearance of light the serpent hid behind. Eve and Adam bought the snake's appealing bill of goods only to discover that all that glitters most certainly wasn't gold at all.

Bent Toward Idolatry

Man has continued his propensity or bent to worship other gods. Think with me for a moment about Moses and the children of Israel. Standing at the brink of certain destruction at the Red Sea, what was their reaction to Jehovah, God Almighty, the great "I AM"? Did they place their confidence in the One Who had overpowered the court magicians? Did they cry out in thanksgiving for the God Who had spared them from the plagues of Egypt, hid them as death passed over, and took the lives of every Egyptian's first born? Did they rest with confidence in Jehovah Who would most certainly be faithful to them once again and deliver them from the hands of the Egyptians? No. They didn't give God a second thought. They resorted to the familiar and the demonic. They trusted in what they could see and feel. They turned their wills and hearts back to the gods and goddess of Egypt and the rulers who had placed them in bondage. Exodus 14:12 says, "...Let us alone that we may serve the Egyptians. For it would have been better for us to serve the Egyptians than that we should die in the wilderness."

They were moments away from God parting the sea before them and swallowing up their enemies. Instead they desired to return to Egypt. Back there they would have to serve Anubis, Horus, Ra and Thoth. They would have to bow their knees and lift their hands to the Earth, sun, sky and moon. They would have to give homage to serpents and vultures, and trust gods and goddesses to bring fertility. They would have to choose idols to sustain their lives instead of the one True and Faithful God. One man decided not to turn and not to serve other gods, but to lead his people to the only One Who could deliver them. Moses declared, in Exodus 14:13, "Do not be afraid. Stand still, and see the salvation of the Lord, which He will accomplish for you today...."

Gods of Our Own Choosing

God wants to be Who He is—God. He will not superimpose His will on ours or force us to do what He knows is in our best interest. He had the power to force every one of the children of Israel to choose Him first, but He didn't. He won't do it with you or me today. I believe that had the Israelites wanted to turn back, God would have let them. Their choice would have brought their destruction. Any time we turn from God to serve idols, judgment and destruction come.

In other countries, unlike here in the United States, those who choose to worship "other gods" find themselves paying a high price. There is no "tolerance." An Associated Press news report out of Ougadougou, Burkina Faso told of villagers who killed a man by burying him alive after accusing him of being a sorcerer. The convicted man, Jean Yameogo, had been discovered digging up an 18-year-old grave to use the bones of the deceased as a fetish. The elders of the village ordered Yameogo to rebury the bones he had removed. The man's son handed him the skeleton bone by bone. When he completed the task, he was beaten and buried alive. In the eyes of the culture, justice had been done.

> God wants to be Who He is—God. He will not superimpose His will on ours or force us to do what He knows is in our best interest.

In contrast, many today are promoting a form of worship that includes anything you determine is your "personal" god. Nothing or no one is exempt. Some call it "religious tolerance." Others say it is the first step toward the coming "one world religion." Either way, it allows the very antithesis of God, the ultimate idol worshiper, the Anti-Christ to emerge onto the scene. *Webster's New Collegiate Dictionary* provides an interesting definition for this new pattern of thinking. It states that tolerance is "the allowable deviation from a standard." What does deviation mean? Webster's says it's "the noticeable or marked departure from accepted norms of behavior."

A lot of people today, including Christians, are having trouble determining what the "standard" is. They are also having trouble distinguishing when there is a "noticeable" departure from the "norm." Many have gotten so far from the truth, that the lie carries more credibility. Jesus said in John 14:6, "I am the way, the truth, and the life. No one comes to the Father except through Me." He didn't say you could take the detour of your choice. He made no provision for multiple paths. He wasn't "politically correct." He didn't say, "All roads lead to Rome," because they don't. Idolatry will get you to "a god" that will never lead you to "the God" and His only Son Jesus Christ.

No Tolerance Policy

Satan laid the groundwork for today's "tolerance" in the Garden when he talked Eve and Adam out of their inheritance. His thinking was "God won't mind. He's a good guy. He loves you. Do what you want. He'll understand."

God says to man. "I made you. I created you to worship Me. I require an undivided heart. I desire worship that exalts no man, no religion, no ideologies, no political agendas, no

> You cannot deal with the objects of idolatry in your home until you deal with the "others gods" in your heart.

systems of thinking and no patterns of behavior. I want you to worship Me and Me alone." Get whatever else is "your god" out of the way. When God said, "You shall have no other gods before Me," He meant it. He did not mean that we could put Him first and then add in other gods after Him. He said, no other gods, period.

You cannot deal with the objects of idolatry in your home until you deal with the "others gods" in your heart. You cannot worship at the throne of celebrity and say you are serving one God. You cannot place those in spiritual authority over you on a pedestal and claim a heart for God alone. You cannot make vows to the pagan gods of freemasonry and serve two masters—God and Satan. Maybe your idols are none of these. Instead, perhaps they are the craving for possessions, position and power.

Gods of the Grid Iron

I remember the day I thought I had no idols until God quickly revealed one of mine. I was preaching on a Sunday morning during the football playoff season. I was anxious to get home. I cut my sermon short, talked to only a few people, and hurried home to watch my favorite team, the Dallas Cowboys. I rationalized my behavior all along the way. After all, didn't most of the men in my congregation want to get home? We all wanted to see the game. That's why attendance had been down. Some didn't show up, afraid they'd miss the opening kickoff.

I was on my way home when God asked me, "Henry, is it important to you that the Cowboys win today?"

"Oh, not really."

"Really," God replied.

"Why lie?" I thought. God knew my heart. "OK, yeah, I want them to win."

"Not only do you want them to win, Henry, but son, they are more important to you than I am."

Ouch. That hurt. But I knew that God had put His finger on my divided heart. They were more important. Everything I had done that day proved it. I asked for God's forgiveness and, of course, He graciously gave it to me. It was a lesson in idolatry that I've never forgotten.

The Masks of Mardi Gras

Several years ago I was asked by a wealthy couple to come and cleanse their home. The wife had been having trouble sleeping and was experiencing an uneasy feeling. We talked briefly when I arrived. I asked them if they were willing to get rid of anything that I identified by the Spirit of God as needing to be removed. They agreed.

As I walked through the downstairs area of this beautiful home, I found nothing remarkable. Everything seemed quite normal. It was only when I started walking upstairs that I began to sense something that wasn't right. When I reached the top of the stairs and started to walk toward the master bedroom, the reason became clear. Along the wall were masks, souvenirs from a trip to Mardi Gras in New Orleans. In the next chapter I will explain that Louisiana's biggest party of the year has deeper roots than drunkenness, nudity and a lot of perverseness.

I told both the husband and his wife that the masks were their house's main problem. Quickly, the husband got a box of trash bags and began disposing of the masks. Once downstairs and outside he crushed them into little pieces, destroying thousands upon thousands of dollars. But it didn't matter. That night he, his wife and the rest of his family slept in peace and have ever since. The cost of his families' freedom was worth the price.

Distorted Images

Remember that idols and everything that brings defilement will take you places you don't want to go. First of all, they will keep you from seeing God the way He really is. When you create a graven image, you distort His image and corrupt His essential nature. Second, you exalt yourself instead of God. Arrogance and pride cost Satan his position in the courts of God. God will not allow any man to exalt himself and be his "own god." The Lord alone will be exalted and lifted up. Third, idolatry leads to sin and immorality. When God is removed from the picture, man resorts to his own nature and carnality. Those that worship "other gods" become obsessed with their own sinful attitudes and lustful desires. Fourth, idols open the door to demonic spirits. When we move from the truth to the lie, we serve the one behind the deception—Satan and his horde of demons. Idolatry will take you farther than you want to go, keep you longer than you want to stay, and cost you more than you want to pay.

Before you look around your home for the statues, occult books, questionable videos, heirlooms or other "obvious idolatrous" objects, take a moment to allow God to search your heart for the altars you have built to other gods and the graven images you have created. Let God remove them from your life and cleanse your heart of the division that has made it difficult for you to serve Him alone. Allow Him to bring you back to the place where no gold glitters, but His glory shines brightly from your life.

Chapter 10

Towers of Power

During the late summer of 2001, one of the leading providers of satellite programming provided its viewers with a free concert series titled, *Music in High Places.* It featured various music groups singing from some of the world's most recognized, spiritually charged New Age locations. In truth, there isn't anything "new" about the "high places" of man's idolatrous worship. Man has been worshiping idols since Eve fell for Satan's 'be your own god" line in the Garden. Trying to keep God first has been man's biggest challenge and one of God's strongest messages to His fallen creation.

Man's Other Gods

It should be no surprise to anyone that God has a problem with idolatry. He's not tolerant of "other gods." The word altar appears in Scripture 55 times in 49 verses, while high altars are mentioned in 13 verses throughout the Old Testament. You don't have to read His lips or get a second opinion. God's very clear. "And God spoke all these words, saying, 'I am the Lord your God, who brought you out of the land of Egypt, out of the house of bondage. You shall have no other gods before Me'" (Exodus 20:1-3). Notice, God didn't say, worship the "gods" of the Egyptians. He didn't suggest that the Israelites summon up a magical "god" from the courts of the Pharaohs and worship it. No. He said, I brought you out of Egypt. I took you out of the house of bondage, worship Me.

In Texas, where I live, we translate it this way: Dance with the one who brought you. Not only does God want our attention, but also He wants our undivided affection and adoration. He has a no-tolerance policy on the worship of "other gods" and the building up of "altars" or "high places." With God, idolatry carries the penalty of judgment and death. Deuteronomy 12:1-4 says, "These are the statutes and judgments which you shall be careful to observe in the land which the Lord God of your fathers is giving you to possess, all the days that you live on the earth. You shall utterly destroy all the places where the nations which you shall dispossess served their gods, on the high mountains and on the hills and under every green tree. And you shall destroy their altars, break their sacred pillars, and burn their wooden images with fire; you shall cut down the carved images of their gods and destroy their names from that place. You shall not worship the Lord your God with such things."

Wickedness in the Earth

When God first contemplated destroying the earth in Genesis 6:5, He "Saw that the wickedness of man was great in the earth, and that every intent of the thoughts of his heart was only evil continually." Verses 6-7 add, "And the Lord was sorry that He had made man on the earth, and He was grieved in His heart. So the Lord said, 'I will destroy man whom I have created from the face of the earth, both man and beast, creeping thing and birds of the air, for I am sorry that I have made them.'"

Imagine! God 's heart was so heavy and broken because of what man had done that He thought it was better to destroy the earth and all His creation. Man's heart, meant to worship and adore God, had turned dark and evil. But God spared one man, his family and two of every kind of creature so that once again He could establish a covenant with man and make a fresh start.

The Tower of Babel

God's second chance for man did not produce the results He desired. Instead of worshiping God alone, man once again chose to worship "other gods" and built a tower into the heavens. The Tower of Babel was built on the plain of ancient Babylon in the southern part of Mesopotamia. Every brick of the massive terraced structure was meant to proclaim the achievement of its builders. They sought to make a name for themselves and to insure that their kingdom would stand.

Babel was devoted to everything human. Man was his own god. Babel's political, economic, educational and religious system exalted man and focused on materialism, defiance, rebellion and idolatry. God could not allow the tower to stand. He caused confusion among the people by changing their one language into many. Verses 6-8 of Genesis 11 says, "And the Lord said, 'Indeed the people are one and they all have one language, and this is what they begin to do; now nothing that they propose to do will be withheld from them. Come, let Us go down and there confuse their language, that they may not understand one another's speech.' So the Lord scattered them abroad from there over the face of all the earth, and they ceased building the city."

> Instead of worshiping God alone, man once again chose to worship "other gods" and built a tower into the heavens.

No high place of man would be allowed to stand. God's judgment had come once again to the idolatrous heart of man. That was not the end, however, of man's idolatry.

Canaan and Their Gods

In Leviticus 26:30 God declares, "I will destroy your high places, [and] cut down your incense altars...." The Old Testament describes these sites of heathen worship as Canaanite sanctuaries. In rural areas, hilltops were set aside as Canaanite high places. In more populated cities, platforms or altars were erected. Various rituals and religious rites were performed as worshipers gave into their animal instincts in worship to pagan gods. Baal, the god of weather and fertility, was the chief god of the Canaanites, driving them to immoral acts with temple prostitutes, bestiality and every form of depravity and evil. Large symbolic stones or massebot in Hebrew were used, along with Asherah poles, graven images, various kinds of vessels, burning incense and raised platforms for human sacrifice. Most of the sacrifices were of children. So stern was Moses' warning to the Israelites before they entered the land of Canaan that Deuteronomy 7:2 declares, "...You shall make no covenant with them nor show mercy to them."

Again in Numbers 33:51-53, God commanded Israel to drive out the idol worshipers before entering the land of promise: "Speak to the children of Israel, and say to them: 'When you have crossed the Jordan into the land of Canaan, then you shall drive out all the inhabitants of the land from before you, destroy all their engraved stones, destroy all their molded images, and demolish all their high places; you shall dispossess the inhabitants of the land and dwell in it, for I have given you the land to possess.'"

Along with God's command came a warning in verse 55-56: "But if you do not drive out the inhabitants of the land from before you, then it shall be that those whom you let remain shall be irritants in your eyes and thorns in your sides, and they shall harass you in the land where you dwell. Moreover it shall be that I will do to you as I thought to do to them."

Israel's High Places

The Israelites had their own high places dedicated to the worship of God. First Samuel 9:12-27 records that Saul met with the prophet Samuel at a high place in the land of Zuph. It would be a day of destiny for Saul. A day before Saul arrived, the Lord spoke to Samuel in verse 16 of 1 Samuel 9 and said, "Tomorrow about this time I will send you a man from the land of Benjamin, and you shall anoint him commander over My people Israel, that he may save My people from the hand of the Philistines; for I have looked upon My people, because their cry has come to Me."

Saul met Samuel at the gate of his house and later both of them went to the high place to talk and eat together. Verse 19 says, "...Go up before me to the high place, for you shall eat with me today; and tomorrow I will let you go and will tell you all that is in your heart."

On another occasion during the reign of Manasseh in 2 Chronicles 33, the people performed sacrifices to God on the high places. After Manasseh's captivity and affliction, he repented before God and took away the foreign gods of the house of the Lord in Jerusalem and repaired the altar and sacrificed peace and thanksgiving offerings. Verses 16-17 say, "He also repaired the altar of the Lord, sacrificed peace offerings and thank offerings on it, and commanded Judah to serve the Lord God of Israel. Nevertheless the people still sacrificed on the high places, but only to the Lord their God." Man just could not stay true to God.

The Lure of the Pagans

During other times, the lure of pagan gods proved to be too strong a temptation. Solomon, during the later part of his reign, built high places outside Jerusalem in honor to the gods of his foreign wives. First Kings 11:7-8 says, "Then Solomon built a high place for Chemosh the abomination of Moab, on the hill that is east of Jerusalem, and for Molech the abomination of the people of Ammon. And he did likewise for all his foreign wives, who burned incense and sacrificed to their gods."

Even after Solomon's death, the idolatry continued until the prophets cried out: "...This is what the Sovereign Lord says: Will you defile yourselves the way your fathers did and lust after their vile images? When you offer your gifts—the sacrifice of your sons in the fire—you continue to defile yourselves with all your idols to this day" (Ezekiel 20:30-31).

"Why are you telling me all of this?" you might be asking. "We don't have idols. We don't bow down to carved images. We're not a bunch of heathens, sacrificing to other gods." Maybe not, but let's look at the origins of a few of America's biggest "holidays" and "celebrations," and you might change your mind.

More Than a Masquerade

Every civilization has its pagan sect or religion. Whether it was Inanna of the Sumerians, Ihtar of the Babylonians, Fortuna of the Romans, Hathor of the Egyptians, Shingmoo of the Chinese, Hertha of the Germans or the "Queen of Heaven" for apostate Jews, all worshiped the creator, mother Earth. Here in America, every year in New Orleans, thousands come to take part in Louisiana's biggest parties—Mardi Gras and the Rio Carnival. Nothing is sacred. The greatest "free for all" party around the world attracts 700,000 partygoers who know no limits.

What's really behind the mask of this anything goes celebration? The masquerade tradition goes back to the Roman aristocracy who looked for opportunities to participate in debauchery and licentiousness. Men put on women's clothing, performed every kind of orgy and carried on a masquerade.

Rome's roots of primitive partying goes a little deeper to more ancient times. In Greece, the god Dionysus was the inventor of revelry. His followers believed in "letting themselves go" and "giving themselves over" to natural, earthly desires. They embraced carnality and its lusts. Wine and every form of perversion helped them to achieve a state of enthousiasmos or being outside their body and inside their god.

Women participated as well, dressing as transvestites, wearing masks, screaming, dancing and engaging in licentious behavior. The "party" atmosphere also included cruelty to people and animals, lesbianism, bestiality, pedophilia and other perversions. Women suckled baby animals that were too young to sense the danger around them. Older animals that tried to escape were torn apart and eaten alive. They threw off every restraint to achieve a state of ecstasy in worship to their god. To resist Dionysus was to bring a curse of terrible madness.

The Hebrews knew a lot about these rituals. They equated Dionysus with the devil and referred to his followers as Bacchants of Hades. He was known as the dark one, who looked like a goat and dwelt in the underworld. They considered those who worshiped him, especially women, to have a satanic connection. Ezekiel describes the magic bands of Dionysis as the kesatot of the Bacchae which was used to capture and imprison the souls of participants. The kesatot was an armband used in connection with a container called a kiste. Both had magic powers.

The kiste in archeological records appears as a sacred vessel with a snake peering through an open lid. Pan is pictured kicking open the lid and allowing snakes to bind women around the limbs and the hair. Exactly how this device imprisoned a person is still a mystery. Ezekiel 13:20 says, "Therefore thus says the Lord God, 'Behold, I am against your magic charms by which you hunt souls there like birds. I will tear them from your arms, and let the souls go, the souls you hunt like birds.'"

> From Mardi Gras to Halloween, idolatry is alive and well. As today's pagans, wiccans take Halloween seriously.

Ezekiel believed that the demon Pan, whose name gave rise to the word pandemonium or "all the devils," imprisoned the souls of men and women through magic and sensuality. That same demonic spirit still strikes panic and pleasure into the hearts of men and beasts every year in New Orleans.

Beyond Trick or Treat

From Mardi Gras to Halloween, idolatry is alive and well. Wiccans take Halloween seriously. As today's pagans, they believe Halloween to be a magic time. Their sabbat celebration represents the final turn of the year-wheel as Mother Earth says her farewell to the god who will be reborn at Yule on December 20. For them it is a time to honor the Earth mother, to remember the ancients and give reverence to the horned god of the Hunt. All Hallows' Eve was first practiced in the 7th century A.D. in remembrance of deceased saints and martyrs. Later changed to November 1, Halloween was "Christianized" to coincide with the pagan holidays of Beltane and Samhain and the festivals of summer, winter and fire.

The real connection to Halloween lies in its ancient and Celtic roots and the goddess Hecate, the Titan Earth mother of the wizards and witches. Derived from the Egyptian word Hecate meaning sorcery and magical, the dark goddess of witchcraft, Isis, was worshiped in impure rites and magical incantations. Her power and influence in the dark world was recognized by many different names. To the Romans, the goddess Trivia, meaning three roads, knew Hecate's worshipers because they practiced magic wherever three paths joined. To the Latin Church, they were recognized as Trivial Pursuit for their journey toward occult knowledge.

As the sorceress of the underworld, Hecate was greatly feared for her ability to afflict the mind with madness, much like the Greek god Dionysus. She also had great influence over the creatures of the night and was thought to govern haunted places where evil or murderous activity occurred.

> Idolatry is all around us in many forms—all deceptive. Believers today must be continually reminded that their heart belongs to only one God, not many.

Her familiar spirit was the night owl who received her oblations on the eve of the full moon. Represented as the combination of a triple-faced dog, snake and horse, she required food offerings known as Hecate's Supper. Her accomplices by night were called strigae and appeared as vicious owl-like creatures who fed on the bodies of unattended babies, but by day looked like simple old women.

The Idols in Our Lives

Idolatry is all around us. It has taken many forms—all deceptive. God is after the idols in our lives. He is serious about our worship of anything other than Him. He will not allow mixture—light and darkness. Believers today must be continually reminded that their heart belongs to only one God, not many. God is crying out to each of us today to turn away from the idols and gods we have chosen to worship instead of Him. We all know who or what our gods are. They are different for everyone.

God Almighty seeks a people who will worship only Him. Serve only Him. Love only Him. God wants voluntary lovers who will give all of their heart, mind, soul, body and spirit to Him alone. Instead of turning to someone else or something else, God says to each of us who will give Him our whole hearts, "I will never leave you. I will never forsake you."

Give Him the towers of power you have built and the other gods you have chosen to worship. Let Him break the high places down until they are reduced to ashes. Then let Him give you "beauty for ashes." Let Him replace your haughtiness with humility and your idolatry with intimacy. Let Him be God—the one God you worship.

Part Three

Rules of
Enforcement

Chapter 11

An Unbreakable Covenant

Today, the word covenant is hard for most people to understand. Few grasp the importance of a binding agreement between people. Most are too accustomed to divorce, breach of contract, and lawsuits. When many people sign on the dotted line of a contract, they are already thinking of ways to get out of it. Hardly anyone today thinks in terms of solemn oaths and lasting covenants especially one that is sealed in blood. That is, except God. He is a covenant making, keeping and revealing God. Even His Word is divided into two testaments or covenants, the Old and the New.

Covenant or the Hebrew word "brit" means a cutting of an agreement or pact made when passing between pieces of flesh. It's a term that was widely used in ancient times. Many cultures used covenants as the basis for interpersonal and social relationships. They existed between nations, among friends, in marriage, as the foundation for a business agreement, and as a set of guidelines for government constitutions.

The First Covenant

God's first covenant with man was made in the Garden of Eden. No other agreement would have been necessary had Adam and Eve stayed within the boundaries of this original covenant. The Edenic Covenant revealed God's purpose for all of creation and for man's dominion and authority. God created the earth to be inhabited. It was never His intention to operate the Earth. He was the owner and desired that His man and woman be the co-operators or managers of the earth. Isaiah 45:18 says, "For thus says the Lord, Who created the heavens, Who is God, Who formed the earth and made it, Who has established it, Who did not create it in vain, Who formed it to be inhabited...." The Edenic Covenant required man to obey God's commands and fulfill His eternal, God-given destiny.

Just like other covenants that would follow later, this covenant had blessings and cursing. In listing the blessings, God said that man, both male and female, would share His image and likeness (Genesis 1:26-27). They would have the ability to recreate themselves. They were commanded to be fruitful and multiply. He wanted His new creation to reproduce themselves both spiritually and physically. He gave Adam and Eve the responsibility and privilege to produce a race of people that would come to know Him, love Him and serve Him for all of eternity (Genesis 1:28). Everything in the earth would now be under their control.

Taking Control

The word "subdue" in Genesis 1:28, indicates that God's new creation would take dominion over the world around them. God expected Adam and Eve to take charge and exercise their authority over the earth and Satan as well.

Satan? Yes, Satan. After Satan's fall from heaven, he was relegated to the second heaven and to the earth where he was looking for an opportunity to gain a foothold. Adam and Eve would soon find out just how serious Satan was about getting control of the earth.

For the time being, all that God had created belonged to man. For the first and last time in their lives, man and woman would get the full cooperation of the entire earth. They were in charge. The animals obeyed them, and the earth yielded its increase providing seeds, herbs and fruit for them to eat. The future looked good.

A Broken Covenant

There was only one catch. Under the terms of God's covenant, man could do anything and have anything, except for the forbidden fruit of the tree of the knowledge of good and evil (Genesis 2:9, 16-17). Every blessing of God belonged to Adam and Eve as long as they obeyed Him. Cursing waited if they were disobedient. Their disobedience would cost them their lives and bring a line of curses on them and all those born after them. The penalty for partaking of the forbidden fruit was the curse of death. Not just physical death, but spiritual death as well. One bite and all that God had provided would be taken from them.

> Before the foundation of the world, God knew that His creation would decide to serve another and hand over their dominion and authority to Satan.

Before the foundation of the world, God knew that His creation would decide to serve another and hand over their dominion and authority to Satan. Their decision would break His heart and cause Him to make the toughest choice imaginable—to sacrifice His only Son to redeem His fallen creation.

Each of us is part of that fallen creation. Even though we didn't actually stand in the Garden with Adam and Eve, we stand every day before God and make the choice for life or death. Deuteronomy declares an eternal challenge for every man and woman. Verse 19 of Chapter 30 says, "I call heaven and earth as witnesses today against you, that I have set before you life and death, blessing and cursing; therefore choose life, that both you and your descendants may live." Make the choice for Jesus and His life today as you pray this prayer.

Lord Jesus, I cannot deny the fact that I have the same choice that my ancestors did. I have the same choice that Adam and Eve had in the Garden. I can choose to believe You and serve You, or believe the lies and deception of Satan and choose death instead of life. Forgive me for my wrong choices, deception and rebellion. Forgive me for choosing to go my own way and ignoring Your truth. Forgive me, Lord, for the times that I have chosen to believe the lies of Satan, rather than the truth of Your Word. Help me to daily choose You and life and not Satan and death. Help me to walk in the reality of Your covenant with me and to receive all the blessings You have made available to me. I acknowledge that all these blessings come to me through Jesus Christ my Lord. Amen.

Chapter 12

Blood for Blood

lood is thicker than water. It's an expression that has been around for centuries and implies a connection so strong that it cannot be severed. Blood is what unifies all mankind. In the realm of the spirit, blood is the essential element. It is the life-sustaining fluid that runs through the arteries and veins of all humans and animals. It is the very core of life itself. To God it is a sacred liquid that contains the gift of life that only He can give.

Leviticus 17:11 says, "For the life of the flesh is in the blood, and I have given it to you upon the altar to make atonement for your souls; for it is the blood that makes atonement for the soul." God made it clear that blood would be required to bring atonement and attain reconciliation with Him.

Signed in Blood

When Adam and Eve gave their authority to Satan and ran from his presence, God killed an animal and clothed His man and woman with its fur. The blood became the sign of the covenants that would bring atonement for the sins of man. God's use of blood established a lasting pattern that would lead to the shedding of His only Son's blood to redeem fallen man.

In the New Covenant—the blood of Jesus Christ—which supersedes all others, blood flows as the key element. Hebrews 9:22 says, "And according to the law almost all things are purified with blood, and without shedding of blood there is no remission." God decided from the start, that blood would be the means to bring cleansing and redemption to all people and all land. "So Christ was offered once to bear the sins of many..." (Hebrews 9:28). Hebrews 10:4 goes on to say, "For it is not possible that the blood of bulls and goats could take away sins."

> Jesus would provide a sacrifice that would be complete and eternal. His body and blood fulfilled all of God's covenants with man.

In the Old Testament, blood is spoken of 360 times. It is the Hebrew word "dam" and refers to bloodshed in war or murder. In the New Testament the word "haima" is used to speak of blood and occurs 99 times. In 39 of those references, the blood of Jesus is mentioned as a sign and seal of the New Covenant. That covenant is the fulfillment of God's plan to provide a perfect sacrifice that would once and for all redeem man and reconcile him to God. Jesus would provide a sacrifice that would be complete and eternal. His body and blood fulfilled all of God's covenants with man.

A Lasting Covenant

The covenant of blood in Jesus Christ brought God and man back together in perfect relationship. It established right-standing. Prior to Jesus, the law required that man atone for his sins through the blood of animals. Each time man sinned, another offering had to be made. There was no lasting remedy and no complete way to wipe away his sin forever. Alfred Edersheim, in his book *The Temple*, records the prayer made by the high priest as he stood over the sin offering: "Ah, Jehovah! I have committed iniquity; I have transgressed; I have sinned—my house and I. Oh, then, Jehovah, I entreat Thee, cover over (atone for, let there be atonement for) the iniquities, the transgressions, and the sins which I have committed, transgressed, and sinned before Thee, I and my house—even as it is written in the law of Moses, Thy servant: 'For, on that day will He cover over (atone) for you to make you clean; for all your transgressions before Jehovah ye shall be cleansed.'"

Detail by detail, the procedure was completed until the sin was atoned. The ceremony foreshadowed the perfect sacrifice that would come. As an additional part of the sacrifice, a scapegoat was chosen. Two goats were placed before the people with their backs turned away. Lots were cast and drawn and placed on each goat. The high priest tied a scarlet cloth to the horn of the goat for Azazel—the scapegoat. The goat designated for Jehovah also received a cloth around its neck signifying that its throat would be cut. Then the scapegoat was turned to face the people waiting for their sins to be placed on him.

The scapegoat presents a clear picture of what happened to Jesus. He was brought before Pilate, a robe was placed on Him, and He was turned and shown to the people. He took their sins on Himself and was led from Pilate's courts to bear all of their iniquities. Tradition has it that when the scapegoat was fully accepted, the scarlet mark became pure white, symbolizing the promise of Isaiah 1:18: "...Though your sins are like scarlet, They shall be as white as snow; Though they are red like crimson, They shall be as wool."

Power in the Blood

So complete is the blood of Jesus, it is the primary weapon that believers use to defeat Satan and every demon from hell. Revelation 12:11 says, "And they overcame him by the blood of the Lamb and by the word of their testimony..." The blood of Jesus gives us right-standing before God, makes us the righteousness of God in Christ Jesus, and answers every accusation the enemy puts against us. It is what gives us the ability to be more than conquerors no matter what the attack.

While Satan lists the charges against us before the throne of God, the blood cries out, "Not guilty!" The blood of Jesus satisfied every complaint, breaks every charge, and provides every word of testimony in our defense. God, through the blood of Jesus, has declared us righteous and victorious in the face of *all* Satan's attacks and accusations.

Every time we remember the covenant that God has made with us through the blood and body of Jesus, we thrust the sword of victory deeper into the core of Satan's strategy against us. Jesus' body declares our wholeness—not only in body, but also of our household, property, possessions and pets. The blood and body of Jesus brings "shalom," or the peace of God, to every cell of our body. It underscores the truth that healing is ours and that nothing is missing and nothing is broken.

> The blood of Jesus satisfied every complaint, breaks every charge, and provides every word of testimony in our defense.

Jesus' blood cleanses us completely from our sins and puts our transgressions as far as the east is from the west. We have become so accustomed to that phrase—"as far as the east is from the west"—we barely know what it really means.

God's Word is perfect and everlasting. Not one portion of it is without significance and meaning. When God said, I will put your sins "as far as the east is from the west," He knew what He was saying. You can get in a plane today and fly south and eventually reach the north. But you can't get in that same plane and reach the west flying east. The east and west never touch. The north and the south always do. God remembers your sins no more. Wherever the blood of Jesus is applied, the results are the same—redemption and cleansing occurs. Not every once in a while, but all of the time. When you apply the eternal blood of Jesus to your sins, circumstances, home, property, possessions, pets and other animals, cleansing comes. Redemption comes. Restoration comes.

Canine Deliverance

The blood of Jesus is our most effective weapon, regardless of the battle we're fighting against Satan—even if it's against one of our pets. I've participated in many house cleanings over the last 12 years, where household pets had been dramatically affected by demonic activity. God touched them and brought freedom, just as He did for their owners. We know from Scripture that evil spirits can inhabit animals and change their behavior. When Jesus cast out the legion of evil spirits from the demoniac of Gadara in Mark 5, they asked permission to enter a herd of pigs. When the demons entered the swine, they caused them to run off a cliff and drown themselves.

When my son and his wife had their first child, my grandson Daniel, I decided to pray over their two chow dogs. My wife, Tina, had become concerned about the natural tendencies of the breed to be aggressive. If you've been around children, you know that they don't think about how they are interacting with an animal. They pull and tug and sometimes antagonize animals without thinking about what kind of response they're going to get.

Chows are interesting dogs. They have a history of being used in eastern temples as guard dogs. These two chows had very different personalities. One, Caleb, was aggressive. The other, Kaya, was proud and haughty. One afternoon I took Caleb, the red chow, the aggressive one, and anointed him with oil. I commanded all spirits of abuse, hurt, fear, death and the killer instinct that caused aggressiveness to leave. He yawned three or four times, slumped to the floor, put his head on his paws and slept for a half hour. I took Kaya, the black chow, and did the same. I commanded the haughty spirit to leave. She opened her mouth wide, yawned three to four times, and slumped to the floor just like Caleb. She put her head on her paws and slept for about one half hour. Neither of the dogs were ever the same.

Feline Freedom

Not long ago, one of my ministry team told me about a series of experiences involving his cat, Frankie. The animal had a particularly laid back personality and wasn't rattled by anything. He was far from the stereotypical "scared cat." Shawn had the cat since he was 6 weeks old, and they'd developed quite a relationship. Frankie was often around when he ministered, and seemed to enjoy deliverance and the presence of God.

One morning, sleeping in after a long night of ministering, Shawn was awakened suddenly. Frankie's not a small cat, so when he jumped up and landed right next to Shawn, it woke him up. The cat was terrified. His tail had increased to three times its natural size. Nothing was visible, but the feeling of a dark, terrifying presence filled the room. Shawn prayed and broke off the spirit of fear and torment and went back to sleep.

Over the next few weeks, similar incidents occurred. Frankie had become a kind of barometer for intrusive attacks by the enemy. Shawn anointed the house, going room to room, commanding all of the 14 root spirits to leave. Total peace returned. He never found out why the spirits had come in. Weeks later, just as a precaution, I walked through Shawn's house and could find nothing. It had been a clear case of intrusion. The best way to deal with intrusion is to deal with it. Don't wait. Use your authority in the Name of Jesus. Expel any and all door crashers who have no legal ground to stay in your life or in your home.

Freedom for All

The blood of Jesus seals God's covenant with each of us that believe. It is an eternal covenant with an unchanging God. He has chosen to recognize the perfect blood of His Son as payment for all that is unholy, ungodly and destructive in our lives. Take a moment, get some bread and some fruit of the vine and remember the power in the covenant of blood that you share with God the Father, His Son Jesus Christ and the Holy Spirit. If you believe that communion should be administered by your priest, pastor or other clergy, you may want to invite him to come and participate with your family. If you're a single parent, partake with your children. If you're single, find a Christian friend to agree with you. Gather your family and experience together the difference that trusting the power of the blood of Jesus can make in your life. Not just today, but every day.

Chapter 13

Recovery Operation

When I was in school there were the three R's—reading, writing and arithmetic. I know. They don't all start with an "r," but they were considered, in my day, as the basics or the building blocks of a good education.

The things I have to share with you in this chapter all start with "r" and have one thing in common—the blood of Jesus. As far as I'm concerned, they are as important as learning how to read, write and do math. These days we have audio books that do your reading for you, computers that correct your spelling and grammar, and calculators that make up for the math you never learned in school. Many believers today are like the "new generation" with the "high tech" tools. They've never really learned the basics and someday they'll need them.

Back to Basics

For the believer, the blood is the foundational building block. It's the basic tool for survival in life, and the difference between victory and defeat. Without the blood of Jesus that provides forgiveness, healing, authority, protection and right-standing with God, we're all sunk. Just like the passengers on the Titanic, without the blood, we're taking a ride on a ship going nowhere but down.

The five "R's" are the steps to taking back what Satan has taken from you. They are the ways and means for recovering all. Just like the 2-5-14 strategy that God gave me for deliverance, these five key concepts combine to form a ready arsenal against the attacks of Satan on your life and home and help you walk in the fullness of God's protection through the blood of Jesus.

Repentance

It literally means to turn away from sin. It's a decision of the will to stop walking in one direction, turn around and walk another way which leads to God. It's a kind of spiritual about-face. Repentance is a change in thinking and attitude that eventually results in a total change of heart. God desires more than our remorse which thinks more about the consequences than the captivity of sin.

Many are the times in all of our lives when we have been like the proverbial "kid caught with his hand in a cookie jar." We didn't have any regret for what we had done, only that we had been caught doing it. Geoffrey W. Bromiley puts it this way in his volume *Theological Dictionary of New Testament Words:* "The result of sin brings remorse, a divinely commissioned call brings repentance." God is looking for our commitment, not just our agreement.

The Rebellion of Saul

The Greek word "metanoia" means an "afterthought and change of mind." God wants us to see the cost of our sin, disobedience and rebellion. He wants to be able to completely erase the effects of our previous decisions and actions. He can only do that when we choose to repent. When we choose to disobey God by doing something He told us not to do or not doing something He told us to do, we build up a "sin" tab that somebody has to pay. Not only that, our disobedience and rebellion opens the door to Satan. First Samuel 15:23

says, "For rebellion is as the sin of witchcraft, And stubbornness is as iniquity and idolatry...."

"Wait a minute," I can hear you saying, "I'm not into witchcraft."

"It is no different to Me," God says. "If you're rebellious or if you're stubborn against Me and My will for your life, it's all the same."

It's still the sin of witchcraft. God takes our disobedience and refusal to repent seriously. Let's take a look at the life of Saul for a minute. In verse 11 of Chapter 15, God tells His prophet Samuel how displeased He is with Saul as king: "I greatly regret that I have set up Saul as king, for he has turned back from following Me, and has not performed my commandments." Instead of turning to God and obeying His commandments, Saul went his own way.

> Like the kid caught with his hand in a cookie jar, we didn't have any regret for what we had done—only that we had been caught doing it.

Earlier in Chapter 15, God had sent Samuel to anoint Saul and give him specific instructions regarding the spoils of his victory over the Amalekites: "The Lord sent me to anoint you king over His people, over Israel. Now therefore, heed the voice of the words of the Lord. Thus says the Lord of hosts: 'I will punish Amalek for what he did to Israel, how he ambushed him on the way when he came up from Egypt. Now go and attack Amalek, and utterly destroy all that they have, and do not spare them. But kill both man and woman, infant and nursing child, ox and sheep, camel and donkey'" (1 Samuel 15:1-3). After the battle, Saul declared when he saw Samuel, "Blessed are you of the Lord! I have performed the commandment of the Lord" (verse 13).

That's strange, Samuel thought when he inquired of Saul in verse 14: "What then is this bleating of the sheep in my ears, and the lowing of the oxen which I hear?" Saul had an answer for Samuel in verse 15: "They have brought them from the Amalekites; for the people spare the best of the sheep and the oxen, to sacrifice to the Lord your God; and the rest we have utterly destroyed."

Without even a breath, Samuel lit into Saul. Verses 16-19 detail his scathing words to Saul reminding him of just Who had put him in charge in the first place–Almighty God. From his first words, "Be quiet!" to his final question, "Why did you swoop down on the spoil, and do evil in the sight of the Lord?" Samuel cuts into Saul's motivations and attitudes. Saul's excuses in verses 20-22 get him nowhere. Saul wanted to break with his words something he had done by his actions. God says that won't work.

When we refuse to repent, Satan just stands and laughs. Obedience with a bad attitude just brings more rebellion. Giving lip service doesn't make it with God. Repentance is not something external. God wants a submitted heart. He requires each of us to own our

> Something happens when we consistently rebel. Over time, it gets easier to sin and the door to Satan and demonic spirits opens wider.

own stuff, admit it and then quit it. When we don't, evil begins to take over our hearts.

Something happens when we consistently rebel. Over time, it gets a little easier to sin and the door to Satan and demonic spirits opens wider. Day by day we walk farther from the light and closer to the darkness. Step by step we lose our freedom, then become captives. By our actions, we box ourselves into a spiritual corner. We get ourselves to the place where we can't escape the consequences of our sin. Whatever we've walked our way into, we'll have to walk our way out of. Jesus provides that way.

An Offering for Sin

Under the conditions of the law, man showed his repentance through a sin offering. Under grace, Jesus became that offering for us. He paid the price that we should have paid. He paid in full our debt of sin. He experienced the wages of sin–death–so that we could experience spiritual life. But in order to receive the forgiveness that comes from

His sacrifice and His blood, we have to repent. We agree with God that we have sinned, and we change our minds about sin. God wants each of us to repent of our sins, turn away from them, and walk toward Him. Only then can the cleansing blood of Jesus bring forgiveness and restore a right relationship between God and us.

A Masonic Connection

A young woman who recently attended one of our seminars, had a strong bloodline connection to divination including, among other things, the practice of freemasonry. The vows, oaths and hidden rituals of freemasonry are undeniably demonic and have roots to the mystery religions of Babylon. Masonic Bibles, robes, rings and other articles used in Masonic rituals carry specific and far-reaching curses and need to be destroyed.

The weekend after the meeting, she discovered her grandfather's Masonic Bible. Paging through it, she discovered prayers, oaths and Masonic symbols mixed in among the scriptures. She decided to burn the Bible. She took it in the backyard and set it on fire. Interestingly enough, only the pages with the occult Masonic prayers, oaths, symbols and other materials burned, leaving the Word of God intact. She had made the choice to repent for the sins of her ancestors. She turned away from the practices of freemasonry and idolatry that were an abomination to God. She did exactly as God prescribes in His Word and burned and destroyed ALL that was against His statues and commandments (Deuteronomy 12:1-3; Acts 19:18-19).

The Nation That Repents

Repentance is not just for individuals. Whole nations need to repent for the sins they have committed. Imagine what the United States of America or your country would be like if neighborhood by neighborhood, city by city, and state by state, we would take seriously the prayer in 2 Chronicles 7:14: "If My people who are called by My name will humble themselves, and pray and seek My face, and turn from their wicked ways, then I will hear from heaven, and will forgive their sin and heal their land." Contained in this verse is a type of conditional promise from the throne of God. God is saying, "If you will do these things, then I will do these other things."

In Chapter 1, I talked about the defilement that has come to the United States of America through incest, adultery, divination, homosexuality and bestiality. Not to mention the sin of abortion that has so penetrated and defiled this land. Even in our sin and rebellion, God calls to His people with this promise and proclamation: He will bless our nation if believers will do several things. Remember, He's not talking to those who have never given their hearts and lives to Jesus. He's not talking to the world. He's talking to believers. He's talking to *His people*. He's talking to those that are called by His Name. He says to them, first, I want you to humble yourself. I want you to be dependent on no one else but Me.

> It's that complete turning, a full repentance and surrender that releases God's promised blessing to hear our prayers, forgive our sin, and heal our land.

That's what humility means. It means to be free from pride and self-effort and totally rely and depend on God. Then God says, "Seek My face. Turn back toward Me. Leave behind those things in your life that have come between us. Repent. Turn from disobedience to obedience. Walk away from rebellion. Develop a heart that desires to love and serve Me. Recommit yourself."

After couples have been married a long time, they often decide to have a second marriage ceremony and recommit themselves to each other. They turn to each other and say their vows, face to face one more time, just to let each other and others know that their commitment is lasting and forever.

God is saying to His people, "Turn and seek My face. Look at Me and commit again all that you are to love, serve and worship Me above anything or anyone." It's that complete turning, a full repentance and surrender that releases God's promised blessing to hear our prayers, forgive our sin, and heal our land.

Agreeing With God

This principle and promise applies when asking God to cleanse your home, property and possessions. You have to be willing to agree with God about the things you've done that have opened the door and given Satan access to your life. Humble yourself. Turn away from the wrongs done in your home. Seek His face and recommit your life and family to Him. He promises to hear, forgive and heal. He is a faithful God Who hears and answers your prayers. He will heal and cleanse your home, land, property and all that you possess. Repent and receive every one of the fruits of your repentance.

Redemption

It's absolutely impossible to have redemption without a redeemer. I particularly like the definition of "redeemer" that appears in the *Revell Bible Dictionary*. A redeemer is a "person who intervenes and pays a necessary price to win the release of another from some bondage or danger." Redemption is God's way of buying back His lost creation. It is His plan for rescuing and delivering mankind. Even though it is fulfilled in the New Testament, redemption has its spiritual roots in the Old Testament as well.

In Hebrew, redemption is the word "padah" and is found 60 times in Scripture including Nehemiah 1:10, Deuteronomy 7:8, Psalm 130:8, Exodus 13:15, and Isaiah 35:10 and 51:11. "Padah" means "to release, preserve, rescue, deliver, liberate, cut loose, to free or ransom." As someone who has ministered in the area of deliverance for the past 30 years, "padah" brings special meaning to Jesus' announcement regarding His earthly ministry in Luke 4:18. He came to bring redemption in all of its fullness. Quoting from the original text in Isaiah 61:1, He declares, "The Spirit of the Lord is upon Me, Because He has anointed Me to preach the gospel to the poor; He has sent Me to heal the brokenhearted, To proclaim liberty to the captives And recovery of sight to the blind. To set at liberty those who are oppressed." God has always, since the Fall of man, wanted to deliver every man and woman from the bondage of sin.

According to the Old Testament, a redeemer was a close relative, blood kinsman or someone in a position of strength who was able to repurchase that which had been lost or stolen by a weaker member of the family. The redeemer could recover property or possessions that had been taken from the helpless and oppressed or victims of violent attack. He could buy freedom for enslaved people. He could obtain dedicated property and livestock that had been allocated for the firstborn. He could serve as the legal avenger when a life had been taken in murder.

Jesus Our Kinsman-Redeemer

Redemption is the central theme of the book of Ruth. In it the concept of a kinsman-redeemer is presented and foreshadows the work of Jesus in the New Testament. Thirteen times throughout the book, the Hebrew word "ga al" is used. Not only does it represent the kinsman-redeemer, but outlines his characteristics. He must be a blood relative to those he redeems. He must be able to pay the price to redeem the person, property, land or possessions. He must be willing to serve as the kinsman-redeemer. He must be a free man.

What a picture this is of Jesus and His work of redemption in all of our lives. In the case of Ruth, Boaz, one of Naomi's kinsmen, provided security and redemption for Ruth by buying back Naomi's land. Boaz also married Ruth and fathered her son. Ruth went from danger to protection, insecurity to security, widowhood to marriage, poverty to wealth, and from being childless to becoming the mother of a bloodline that eventually led to David, the root of Jesse—the bloodline of "The Redeemer, Jesus Christ."

Jesus Christ is our kinsman-redeemer by His blood. He delivers each of us from sin, the oppression of the enemy, and death itself. First Peter 1:18-19 says, "Knowing that you were not redeemed with corruptible things, like silver or gold, from your aimless conduct received by tradition from your fathers, but with the precious blood of

Christ, as of a lamb without blemish and without spot." Ephesians 1:7 declares, "In Him we have redemption through His blood, the forgiveness of sins, according to the riches of His grace." The blood of Jesus secures our release. His blood pays our ransom. Mark 10:45 says, "For even the Son of Man did not come to be served, but to serve, and to give His life a ransom for many." We are set free from the captivity of sin by His blood. Slaves no more to Satan; we are bond slaves to a new master, Jesus Christ. His blood has become the key that unlocks the prison doors to our hearts and lives.

> We are set free from the captivity of sin by Jesus' blood. Slaves no more to Satan, we are bond slaves to a new master, Jesus Christ.

Not one of us is without the need for His redeeming blood. Romans 3:23-26 says, "For all have sinned and fall short of the glory of God, being justified freely by His grace through the redemption that is in Christ Jesus, whom God set forth as a propitiation by His blood, through faith, to demonstrate His righteousness, because in His forbearance God had passed over the sins that were previously committed, to demonstrate at the present time His righteousness, that He might be just and the justifier of the one who has faith in Jesus."

The Reality of Redemption

The blood of Jesus has the power to completely release, preserve, rescue, deliver, liberate, cut loose, sever, free and ransom every part of our lives, family, nations, and individual homes, property, land and possessions. Allow the blood of the One Who "sticks closer than a brother," the kinsman-redeemer Jesus Christ to take back for you everything you have lost spiritually, emotionally, financially, relationally and physically.

Galatians 4:1-6 says, "Now I say that the heir, as long as he is a child, does not differ at all from a slave, though he is master of all, but is under guardians and stewards until the time appointed by the father. Even so we, when we were children, were in bondage under the elements of the world. But when the fullness of the time had come, God sent forth His Son, born of a woman, born under the law, to redeem those who were under the law, that we might receive the adoption as sons. And because you are sons, God has sent forth the Spirit of His Son into your hearts, crying out, 'Abba, Father!' What a great thing to know that no matter what kind of trouble you're in, Daddy can help you through it. Today, reach out and receive the fullness of your redemption and adoption as a child of God.

> God's form of justice requires complete and comprehensive restitution and it is satisfied by the "once and for all" payment of His Son's blood.

Restitution

The Law of Moses wasn't soft on crime. Restitution was required for wrong doing, plus some added interest. It wasn't just a matter of hiring the best attorney you could find and getting a reduced sentence of community service. I've got nothing against lawyers. Some of my friends practice law. But our present system is not the justice of Moses' day.

In Hebrew, the word restitution, used in Numbers 5:7-8, is "sub," which means to turn back or return. When someone wronged another person, they first had to confess their sin and then pay the wronged party the full monetary value plus a penalty. Sometimes that was 20 percent, other times double. "Then he shall confess the sin which he has committed. He shall make restitution for his trespass in full, plus one-fifth of it and give it to the one he has wronged. But if the man has no relative to whom restitution may be made for the wrong, the restitution for the wrong must go to the Lord for the priest, in addition to the ram of the atonement with which atonement is made for him" (Numbers 5:7-8).

The Old Testament cites another word for restitution used in both Exodus 22 and Leviticus 22. The word "salam" is similar to the

Hebrew word "shalom," which means nothing missing and nothing broken, but deals more specifically with the restoration of a damaged relationship via monetary payments. Think about all of the broken or damaged relationships you've had and then attach a dollar figure to them plus penalties. That might make each of us think a little more about the way we handle our relationships with others.

Even though restitution exists in civil law, it doesn't carry the punch and power of Mosaic law. Under Old Testament law, restitution is critical and absolute. Whether murder or theft, restitution must be made. When blood has been shed, blood is the payment. When theft or misuse of property is the crime, repayment must be made directly to the victim.

Somebody Has to Pay

Restitution doesn't come cheap. In Moses' day, guilty parties didn't spend a lifetime in jail like they do today without making restitution to the victims or their families. What if you as an individual had to make restitution for all the wrongdoing of every person on the face of the earth from the Garden of Eden to the present moment? Keep in mind that you'd have to be able to return everything plus an additional penalty of at least 20 percent if not double.

God's justice is pay up in full, now! That's the deal. No plea-bargains, no possibility of parole, no suspended sentence. That's justice on heaven's terms. That is, without Jesus.

Restitution for the broken covenants, beginning in the Garden of Eden and including every covenant thereafter, can be satisfied by only one—Jesus Christ. God's form of justice requires complete and comprehensive restitution and it is satisfied by the "once and for all" payment of His Son's blood. The reality of Jesus' blood to pay all our debt plus interest should be a constant reminder of His amazing grace and love for each one of us. We have been forgiven a great debt that we can never repay.

How quickly we seek mercy for ourselves, but justice for others. We want full restitution for us, but look for a way out when dealing with others. We seek out every point of law to argue our case against others, but scan every page of case law for our legal loophole.

An Unpayable Debt

Jesus told a parable of reconciliation, restitution and forgiveness in Matthew 18:21-35. While Peter was looking for his own spiritual loophole regarding forgiveness "under the law," Jesus was shining the light on his heart's motivations. Peter wanted to do only what was the bare minimum under the law by forgiving an offender seven times. Jesus challenged him with verse 22 of Chapter 18: "I do not say to you, up to seven times, but up to seventy times seven." For years I thought Jesus was saying, "Keep a list. When you total up 490 offenses against a person, you don't have to forgive them any more." I found out later what Jesus meant when he made mention of 70 times seven.

According to Jesus, a person would have to sin against you 490 times for the same sin, on the same day. So just to accomplish this feat, a person would have to sin, repent and sin again every 2.6 minutes for 24 hours. That's impossible! Jesus had just raised the mark of true forgiveness to the highest possible level. Then he told Peter and the rest of the disciples a story about two men, both that had debts they couldn't pay.

The Unjust Servant

The king had a servant with a debt of 10,000 talents. At the time, a talent was a weight and measure that calculated precious metals of gold and silver. Considering the price of gold on the market today ($400 per ounce), the servant would have owed the king more than $20,176,000. That's a lot of debt! Based on servant's wages, he would have had to work for 50 years saving every bit of money he made. His lifetime wages of more than $486,000 wouldn't even have put a dent in his unpayable debt!

The king had mercy on him and forgave his debt and sent him on his way. Once he got home, he forgot what had just happened. He accosted one of his fellow servants who owed him 100 denarii, which today would be equivalent to $12.50. He had no mercy and refused to forgive his fellow servant, but threw him into prison. Two servants watching what had happened exposed the servant's evil heart to the king. The king, angered by his servant's actions, required him to pay everything he owed him.

We have a debt we can never pay. To make restitution to God for all our sin and wrongdoing would be like paying off a $20 million debt. That's not even counting taxes and penalties. Yet God tells us that someone else has paid our debt for us. Another has made restitution and His Name is Jesus. He paid our debt. Now He asks us to do what He told Peter to do—forgive.

> To make restitution to God for all our sin and wrongdoing would be like paying off a $20 million debt.

Remember how much you have been forgiven and forgive and make restitution. Make things right in your relationships. Take the effort to return things to the way they were before the damage was done. Then God will bring restoration.

Restoration and Reclamation

It's a compelling story of loss, restoration, and reclamation that starts at Genesis and works its way all through Scripture to Revelation. God had a plan from before the foundation of the earth to restore everything that mankind would lose at the Fall. It starts with the blood of an animal to clothe the first man and woman, and continues to the Second Coming of Jesus Christ to rule and reign and make a new heaven and new Earth that will remain for all time and eternity.

The thread that runs all the way through from the first page of the Word of God to the last is the blood. His blood makes all things new and is available to every believer. Just as Jesus' blood works in our lives and transforms us from death to life and from old creatures to new ones, He touches everything inside and outside of our lives.

Recovering All

First Samuel 30 records the story of the Amalekites that invaded Ziklag and burned it with fire, taking captive all the women, sons, daughters and possessions. When David returned with his troops, all that was his was held captive. The people around him were so angry that they contemplated stoning him to death.

In the midst of chaos, David didn't panic. He sent for the priest and the ephod and asked the Lord what he should do. Verse 8 says, "So David inquired of the Lord, saying, 'Shall I pursue this troop? Shall I overtake them?' And He answered him, 'Pursue, for you shall surely overtake them and without fail recover all.'" God wanted David to go and recover, not part, but all.

God says to each of us today, receive My restoration. Take the blood of My only Son, Jesus Christ, and go and recover ALL that the enemy has taken. Go and reclaim what's yours. The blood of Jesus has taken back all that Satan has stolen from you. Now you go in His power and His authority and get it.

> The blood of Jesus has taken back all that Satan has stolen from you. Now you go in his power and his authority and get it.

I believe it's long past time for all of us to get what's ours. Just after the Civil War, Abraham Lincoln, as a part of the Emancipation Proclamation, gave 40 acres and a mule to each former slave to begin their lives as free men. Do you know that the majority of slaves never claimed what was theirs?

Jesus has reclaimed ALL of your life. He has released, rescued, liberated and cut loose EVERYTHING that the enemy has held in his possession. Receive all that Jesus has ransomed for you. You are no longer a slave to Satan. Receive your redemption and your freedom as a bond slave to Jesus Christ.

Chapter 14

Ground Zero–
Cleaning Up

Cleanliness is not next to godliness.
But sometimes we think it is. I remember at least one Sunday morning
when my wife dressed my son for church and found him minutes later
covered in dirt from head to toe. We could have taken him to church
in that condition. God wouldn't have minded, but we did. So we took
him back in the house, pulled off his dirty clothes, and put on some
clean ones. That's a lot like what God does for us. He takes the dirt,
mud and crud out of our lives, and cleans us up. When my son was
that age, he wouldn't have been good at getting himself "cleaned up."
No matter what our age, as far as God is concerned, we still can't do a
good enough "clean up job" on ourselves. That's a job for God alone.

The Undefiled

The biblical concept of clean and unclean, holy and unholy, is found
in the understanding of several Hebrew words and the practices
behind them. The first word "naqi" or innocent is found 94 times in
the Old Testament and means "to be, or become clean." Another
closely associated word "taher" appears 204 times and means "ritual

or moral cleanness." It also is used to suggest a pure metal that has no alloys. On the opposite side of the coin, the word "tame," which is mentioned 279 times, means to be "unclean or defiled." In Leviticus and Numbers it refers to ceremonial or ritual uncleanness. Later in Ezekiel it is used to describe moral impurity or pollution. The Hebrew word "taher," in all of its forms, occurs 204 times. Most of the time it refers to instructions to the priests in Leviticus and Numbers. It also appears in Exodus, Chronicles and Ezekiel. In the book of Nehemiah it speaks of the moral condition of a nation.

Regardless of the usage, cleansing in the Old Testament focuses on ritual, moral purity and holiness that separate God's people for worship to Him alone. Those who served as priests, all places, sacrificial animals and objects of worship had to be holy and consecrated to God, set apart for His use. In Old Testament times, menstruation, some skin diseases, the afterbirth from a woman's womb, touching a dead person, and certain foods and animals made a person unclean (Genesis 7:2, 8:20; Deuteronomy 14:3-21; Leviticus 11-15; Numbers 19). While uncleanness did not invalidate a person's relationship with God under Mosaic law, it did disrupt it temporarily. The law provided certain steps to follow to become pure and clean again and restore right relationship with God and others.

By the Law

The Mosaic law described a lifestyle pattern prescribed by God. Sinful acts defiled a person and made them unclean. Psalm 24:3-4 declares, "Who may ascend into the hill of the Lord? Or who may stand in His holy place? He who has clean hands and a pure heart, Who has not lifted up his soul to an idol, Nor sworn deceitfully." Sin created an inner defilement of the heart. Men chose, as the psalmist said, to make themselves unclean by what they chose to participate in. Their idolatry and hardened hearts toward God brought pollution to themselves and their land.

In Genesis 35, God instructs Jacob to cleanse his house of foreign gods and take his entire household to a new place. "And Jacob said to his household and to all who were with him, 'Put away the foreign gods that are among you, purify yourselves, and change your garments. Then let us arise and go up to Bethel; and I will make an altar there to God, who answered me in the day of my distress and has been with me in the way which I have gone" (verses 2-3).

The prophet Jeremiah delivers a scathing sermon to Israel over their idolatry in Chapter 2:17-19: "Have you not brought this on yourself, In that you have forsaken the Lord your God When He led you in the way? And now why take the road to Egypt, To drink the waters of Sihor? Or why take the road to Assyria, To drink the waters of the river? Your own wickedness will correct you, And your backslidings will rebuke you. Know therefore and see that it is an evil and bitter thing That you have forsaken the Lord your God, And the fear of Me is not in you,' Says the Lord God of hosts." Verse 22 adds, "'For though you wash yourself with lye, and use much soap, Yet your iniquity is marked before Me,' says the Lord God." No matter how severe the outward cleansing, it was not enough to wash clean the defilement of Israel's worship to other gods.

> The Law provided certain steps to follow to become pure and clean again and restore right relationship with God and others.

The continued practice of immorality and idolatry prompted the prophet Micah to declare God's judgment on Israel and the land in Chapter 2, verses 1-2: "Woe to those who devise iniquity, And work out evil on their beds! At morning light they practice it, Because it is in the power of their hand. They covet fields and take them by violence, Also houses, and seize them. So they oppress a man and his house, A man and his inheritance."

Sin, like a lie that develops a life of its own, has a domino effect. The sin of one can affect even a whole nation as Haggai 2:13-14 says, "'If one who is unclean because of a dead body touches any of these, will it be unclean?' So the priests answered and said, 'It shall be unclean.' Then Haggai answered and said, 'So is this people, and so is this nation before me,' says the Lord, 'and so is every work of their hands; and what they offer there is unclean.'"

It's Only Temporary

Even as the prophets cried out about the sins of the people before God, they knew that ceremonial cleansing provided only a temporary solution. The Day of Atonement provided the way to cleanse the people from their sins. Leviticus 16:30 says, "For on that day the priest shall make atonement for you, to cleanse you, that you may be clean from all your sins before the Lord." Cleansing was not just a ritual; it was a matter of the heart.

One instance of this occurs when Hezekiah the king sent out a proclamation to all of Israel and Judah, stretching from Beersheba to Dan. He declared in 2 Chronicles 30:5 "...They should come to keep the Passover to the Lord God of Israel at Jerusalem, since they had not done it for a long time in the prescribed manner." When the multitude of the people from Ephraim, Manasseh, Issachar and Zebulun came, they had not cleansed themselves. Verses 18-20 of Chapter 30 say, "...Yet they ate the Passover contrary to what was written. But Hezekiah prayed for them, saying, 'May the good Lord provide atonement for everyone who prepares his heart to seek God, the Lord God of his fathers, though he is not cleansed according to the purification of the sanctuary.' And the Lord listened to Hezekiah and healed the people."

Despite their ritual and moral uncleanness, God looked at the sensitivity of their hearts and received, cleansed and healed them. That was the real issue with Him. God was looking for a people who would give their hearts to Him in worship.

Changing Hearts Forever

The prophets looked to the One Who would provide a lasting, supernatural work that would cleanse and change the hearts of men forever. Jesus provided that full and complete atonement. His greatest critics, the Pharisees, were stuck on ritual details. They obsessed and nitpicked the law. They had difficulty understanding the difference between outward cleansing and inward purity and its relationship to worship. They complained that Jesus and His disciples ate with unclean hands—a local tradition, not a Mosaic law. Jesus said this to them in Matthew 23:24-28, "Blind guides, who strain out a gnat and swallow a camel! Woe to you, scribes and Pharisees, hypocrites! For you cleanse the outside of the cup and dish, but inside they are full of extortion and self-indulgence. Blind Pharisee, first cleanse the inside of the cup and dish, that the outside of them may be clean also. Woe to you, scribes and Pharisees, hypocrites! For you are like whitewashed tombs which indeed appear beautiful outwardly, but inside are full of dead men's bones and all uncleanness. Even so you also outwardly appear righteous to men, but inside you are full of hypocrisy and lawlessness." Jesus was telling all who would hear to avoid the defilement of Pharisaical thinking and actions. Traditionally, tombs were whitewashed so that those walking by would not touch them and defile themselves.

> When our heart is His, all of the rest of the outside, those things that affect our everyday life, will come into line.

What a great message that is for us today. Jesus wants us to allow Him to cleanse the inside. When our heart is His, all of the rest of the outside, those things that affect our everyday life, will come into line. His blood has washed us clean. Now He says to each of us, don't defile yourselves with patterns of thinking that lead to wrong actions and develop demonic strongholds in your life.

As you begin the process of allowing God to cleanse your home, property and possessions, ask Him to reveal the hidden things of darkness that crowd Him out of your heart. Instead of your heart being marked with the "whitewash" of defilement, allow Him to wash it with His blood.

Remember David's prayer. This man, who was dearly loved by God, sinned against God. He committed both adultery and murder, and lied to cover the evil actions of his heart. After the prophet Nathan exposed his sin, David prayed. Let his prayer be yours as you seek God's cleansing.

Have mercy upon me, O God, according to Your lovingkindness according to the multitude of Your tender mercies, blot out my transgressions. Wash me thoroughly from my iniquity, and cleanse me from my sin (Psalm 51:1-2). Create in me a clean heart, O God, and renew a steadfast spirit within me. Do not cast me away from Your presence, and do not take Your Holy Spirit from me. Restore to me the joy of Your salvation, and uphold me with Your generous Spirit. Then will I teach transgressors Your ways, and sinners shall be converted to You. Amen (Psalm 51:10-13).

Part Four

Opening Portals

Chapter 15

Making Connection

Not long ago, my wife made plans for a new house. God has greatly blessed us over the 40 years of our life together in marriage and in ministry. He has a particular timetable that I'm not sure we fully understand. About every 12 years or so, He moves us on to another home. So, right on time, He opened the doors for us to build a house. And we laid the foundation. I have some background in the construction business so I know you can't start framing a house, applying sheet rock or putting in windows before you lay the foundation.

Before you start cleansing your home, I want you to make sure that you have laid the right foundation for your life–Jesus Christ. He is the chief cornerstone. When we build our lives on Him and His Word, we have a structure that will stand against the storms of life. Jesus talked about that in Matthew 7:24-25 at the end of His sermon on the mount: "Therefore whoever hears these sayings of Mine, and does them, I will liken him to a wise man who built his house on the rock: and the rain descended, the floods came, and the winds blew and beat on that house; and it did not fall, for it was founded on the rock." The house of our lives will stand strong when we build it on Jesus Christ and His Word.

A Strong Foundation

Several years ago, I heard an interesting story about a woman who bought her first home. During the first conversation she had with the building superintendent she asked that he place one of her personal, marked Bibles in the foundation. He agreed and they decided that the Bible would be set into the concrete just about two feet or less inside the front threshold. Once the foundation was laid and the framing had begun, she went in, prayed, anointed the house, and put scriptures on every wall, floor and step of the house. Interestingly enough, later she discovered that some people in the development had experienced severe shifting and even cracking of their foundations. But her home was solid as a rock. Her foundation was strong. It wasn't so much that she had placed the actual Bible in the foundation that had produced that result, but her life was built on the rock of Jesus and His Word.

Built Upon the Rock

If you don't know Jesus as your personal Lord and Savior, I want you to pray this prayer right now with me. Wherever you are, say this out loud. I like to tell people, say it loud enough for Satan and every demon in hell to hear you.

Lord Jesus, I realize that I was born separated from You, dead in my sins. I have lived in rebellion to Your will. My life has been filled with sinful choices. I have no hope of freeing myself or forgiving myself. Without You I will be forever lost. Thank You for dying for my sins and rising again to buy me from slavery. I believe that Your sacrifice is sufficient and complete. I repent of my rebellion to Your authority. I give my life to You trusting Your salvation. Come into my life and make me a new creation. Thank You, Lord Jesus, for giving me Your free gift of salvation. Amen.

If you prayed this prayer, trusting Jesus with your whole heart, you're now a member of God's family. You are His child and a joint heir with Jesus Christ. God has established a covenant with you, an everlasting agreement that is sealed in the blood of Jesus. Now you can make this declaration.

> Heavenly Father, I thank You that I have been bought and paid for by the blood of Jesus Christ. And because I have been bought and paid for, I am an heir of God and a joint heir with Jesus. As a joint heir, I live in Jesus and He lives in me. And because He lives in me, I have the right to overcome because He overcame. Now as an overcomer, I break every evil curse, spell, hex or demonic assignment that has come into my life and entered my home. I take these curses, spells, hexes and assignments and nail them to the Cross and appropriate the power of the Cross in breaking their power over my life and my household. Your Word says Jesus was made a curse for me, so any curses, spells, hexes or other assignments that come to me and my household, including my home and all of my land, possessions and pets, must come through the blood of the Cross and the blood of the Cross will transform them from a curse into a blessing.
>
> With an act of my will, I choose to receive every blessing that You, heavenly Father, have for me. Now I take back any ground that I have ever given any demonic spirit, whether knowingly or unknowingly. I renounce all contact with anything occultic or satanic. I cut all ungodly ties with any previous owners or possessors of this land, home, possession or pets. I declare that no evil spirit has any right to me or my household. I declare them defeated in every area of my life, home, land, possessions and pets. I have authority in the Name of Jesus. I cut all chains and break all bands. In the Name of Jesus Christ, I bind you and cast you out now. You have no place or memorial in me and my household or in this house, on this land, among my possessions, or over my pets. I pull down every stronghold in the mighty Name and authority of Jesus Christ, by His resurrection power and the power of the Cross. Satan, you and your demons are defeated and your power broken this day in my life and in my household.

Chapter 16

Two Are Better
Than One

Remember for a moment the last time you had a disagreement with someone. Maybe you never raised your voice. You might have even heard their point of view. Somewhere along the way, you probably reached some common ground or simply agreed to disagree. In the natural, that's workable. But not in the things of the spirit.

God puts the question this way in Amos 3:3: "Can two walk together, unless they are agreed?" Jesus promised some powerful results when people are in agreement. Even though Jesus is talking about the actions that must take place to remedy an offense between two believers, His words have even more far-reaching implications. In Matthew 18:18-19, He says, "Assuredly, I say to you, whatever you bind on earth will be bound in heaven, and whatever you loose on earth will be loosed in heaven. Again I say to you that if two of you agree on earth concerning anything that they ask, it will be done for them by My Father in heaven."

The Greek word that Jesus used in this passage is "symphoneo." It's like our word for symphony and means to "sound together, or be in accord, or harmony." Power comes from heaven when we pray in agreement together. God does not ignore the prayers of those who seek His face and join together to exercise their agreement and their faith.

As you gather together as husband and wife, as a family, or as a single person with friends for the cleansing of your home and all that God has given you, know that God will honor your coming together in agreement.

God's Dwelling Place

Dedicate your home to the Lord today. Even as you have given your heart to Him as a dwelling place, now present your home and property to Him as a habitation. Acknowledge any sin you have or any wickedness, evil spirits or unholy atmosphere that you have allowed into your home. Tell God that you are willing to remove everything that separates you from Him. Agree to honor God by filling your home with atmosphere, activities and objects that bring Him glory. Dedicate your home, land, possessions and pets to Him. Set everything you have apart for Him and Him alone.

Pick a central place in your home, join hands and have the head of the household or the person in authority in the home make this dedication. As the prayer is made, agree together that God, by His power and through the body and the blood of Jesus and the working of the Holy Spirit, will accomplish it according to His promise and His Word.

Father, You are the Lord of my Life. Thank You that I have chosen to make You my refuge and my dwelling place, a strong tower and a mighty fortress. Now I ask You, in the Name of Jesus and by the power of the Holy Spirit, to come and receive my home and all that I possess. I give them to You. I ask You to search and find any hidden thing that has brought sin, wickedness, evil spirits or an unholy atmosphere into my home, land, possessions and pets. Come, Lord Jesus, apply Your body and Your blood. Break the power of the enemy in every room of this home, on every possession and object, on the heads of my animals, and on every portion of my land and property. Come, Lord Jesus, remove all evil from this place. Then, Lord, fill my home with Your presence and use it for Your purposes. Set it apart for Your use alone. Send Your angels to the doors, the gates and around the boundaries to shield and protect all that You have given me. Protect this home and land from all evil, pestilence, sickness, disease and destruction of every kind. I declare that this home, land, property, and all my possessions and pets are Yours. I am simply a steward overseeing everything You have placed within my hands. This household will serve You alone. You are my strong habitation. I turn to You at all times. I trust in You. You are my shield and buckler, my salvation, my high tower, my fortress, my refuge and my rock. Evil has no place here. You are my deliverer. Thank You, Lord. In Jesus' Name. Amen.

Chapter 17

Undefiled—Cleansing Your Home

Now it's time to walk through each room of your house, starting with the front door and ending up in the garage. As part of the cleansing, you will also want to go outside and stake your property, draw new boundaries and cleanse the land. I'll be giving you more information on those steps in a later chapter.

I believe that whenever God removes a curse He pronounces a blessing. So when I go through a room, I remove evil and replace it with God's promised blessing.

The Front Door—Threshold

Let's start with the front door. As the head of the household and the authority, anoint the doorposts and pray.

> Lord Jesus, I present this land, property, home and all the inhabitants of this household, with its possessions, to You. I say this day that as for me and my house, we will serve the Lord. Now come and break every hex, vex, spell, evil spirit and demonic assignment from this land, property and home. Remove every

spirit of infirmity, fear, divination, whoredom/idolatry, bondage, haughtiness, perverseness, deaf and dumbness, heaviness, lying, anti-Christ, stupor, error and jealousy by the power and authority of Your blood and Your Name. Build a strong tower in the middle of this home. Make this a place of refuge and a habitation for Your presence and Your glory. Bless us with Your peace, protection and prosperity. Bring the blessings of Deuteronomy 28:1-13 on our work, our children, our provision, our finances and our relationships. May we be blessed coming in and going out. Thank You, Lord, for Your anointing, blessing and presence in this house, in Jesus' Name. Amen.

Remember that this is a typical cleansing that addresses the major rooms in an average home. I cannot possibly address every floor plan. The principles for the rooms that I cover can be adapted to your home.

The Formal Dining Room
As you walk into the room, anoint the doorway and the windows. Then look around the room for any artwork, objects or furniture. Carefully examine these for the artistic patterns we discussed earlier. Then pray over the room.

Lord Jesus, break any and all demonic assignments on this room and the objects here. Cleanse them for Your purposes. Keep all anger, strife, broken relationships and all evil away from this room. Gather people around this table for fellowship, friendship and encouragement. May the conversations that take place here bring peace, healing and comfort to all who sit here, and glory to Your Name. I declare that all food eaten here will nourish the body and no death or poison will be in the food. In Jesus' Name. Amen.

The Kitchen and Breakfast Dining Area
Anoint the doorways and windows in this room. Take a minute to look through your pantry and cupboards for anything that might catch

your attention. It could be a plate with an unusual design or a vase passed down from a grandmother. Whatever it is, ask the Holy Spirit to specifically tell you what action to take regarding the item. Remember, not all objects need to be removed or destroyed. But you do need to be willing to do what the Holy Spirit prompts you to do and what is clearly outlined in the Word of God. Then pray this:

> Lord Jesus, break any and all demonic assignments on this room and the objects here. Cleanse them for Your purposes. Keep all anger, strife, unforgiveness and broken relationships from this place where we come every day for meals. Fill this room with Your presence, peace and protection each morning before we go our separate ways. Help us to keep You first in all that we do. Lord, break every spirit of fear, poverty, lack and the blocking of our success from this place. Remove every obstacle to the blessings You have for our family. Help us to remember that You alone are our provider no matter what situation we are in. Now come, Lord Jesus, and bless us according to Your Word. May the pantry and the cupboards always be full and may we have a willing and obedient heart to share our abundance with others. We bless all food eaten in this place to nourish our body. In Jesus' Name. Amen.

The Living Room or Den

As you have done with other rooms, anoint the doorway and windows. Because this room is generally an area where families relax and enjoy free time, look over all media that might need prayer or removal. Also check all artwork, furniture and other objects just like you've done in the other rooms of the house. Don't be in a hurry. Continue to be sensitive to hear the voice of the Holy Spirit as you walk around the room. When you feel peace in your spirit and know that you're ready, pray this prayer:

> Lord Jesus, break any and all demonic assignments on this room and the objects here. Cleanse them for Your purposes. Keep all anger, competition, jealousy, hurt, and unforgiveness from this

room as we relax and enjoy our time with each other and with friends. Close every door to evil. Help us to put a watch over what we see with our eyes, hear with our ears and say with our mouths. Remove all fear, bondage, divination, whoredom/idolatry, perverseness, heaviness, lying and jealousy from this place. We ask You to close any and all doors to the enemy that we have opened here. Give us wisdom regarding the entertainment we participate in including television, videos, music, games and other media. In Jesus' Name. Amen.

The Bedroom

When praying for each bedroom in your home, be specific. Bedrooms are places of privacy, intimacy and rest. Listen carefully to the Holy Spirit as you pray for your bedroom as husband and wife, for the rooms your children sleep in and for guestrooms where friends and family stay when they visit. If you know of problems or difficulties a member of your family has faced or is struggling with, pray regarding that when you get to their room. Look at artwork, objects and furniture and make sure they are free of questionable influences. Then pray the appropriate prayer.

The Master Bedroom—Husband and Wife

Lord Jesus, break any and all demonic assignments on this room and the objects here. Cleanse them for Your purposes. Keep all anger, jealousy, hurt, unforgiveness, divorce and division from this room and our relationship. Help us to remember to reconcile every difference between us before we sleep each night so that we give the enemy no place in our lives and relationship. Remove and cut off every assignment of whoredom, adultery, rape, lust, seduction, pornography, masturbation, harlotry, illegitimacy, exhibitionism, multipartner orgies, bestiality, perverseness and all sexual sins from us. We declare this marriage bed is set apart, sanctified, holy unto You, God. Bless our covenant and increase our love, devotion, communication, and intimacy with each other day by day and year by year. We welcome You into our times of intimacy together and ask that You make them times of love for each other and worship to You. Thank You for sealing this place with Your presence, peace, love and rest, in Jesus' Name. Amen.

The Master Bedroom—Single Man or Woman

Lord Jesus, break any and all demonic assignments on this room and the objects here. Cleanse them for Your purposes. Keep all loneliness, depression and lying spirits from me. Remove and cut off every assignment of whoredom, fornication, adultery, rape, lust, seduction, pornography, masturbation, harlotry, illegitimacy, exhibitionism, multipartner orgies, bestiality, perverseness and all sexual sins. I declare myself and this bed set apart, sanctified, holy unto You God. Bless me and keep me pure until You bring the one that You have chosen for me in marriage into my life. I welcome You into this time of singleness and ask You to increase my devotion, love, intimacy and worship for You. Thank You for sealing this place with Your presence, peace, love and rest, in Jesus' Name. Amen.

The Bedroom—Infant, Child, Young Adult

Lord Jesus, break any and all demonic assignments on this room and the objects here. Cleanse them for Your purposes. Keep all loneliness, depression and lying spirits from (insert their names). Remove and cut off every assignment against their destiny including every generational, bloodline spirit of infirmity, bondage, fear, divination, whoredom/idolatry, haughtiness, perverseness, anti-Christ, deaf and dumbness, heaviness, lying, jealousy, slumber and error and any assignment of death. I have dedicated (him or her) to You and declare (him or her) set apart, sanctified, holy unto You God. Draw (him/her) to You. I will continue to train (him or her) in the way they should go and I am trusting You Lord to keep (him or her) in all Your ways that (he or

she) will not depart from You. Keep (him or her) pure until You
bring the one that You have for (him or her) to marry. Thank You
for sealing this place with Your presence, peace, protection, rest
and love, in Jesus' Name. Amen.

The Guestroom

Lord Jesus, break any and all demonic assignments on this
room and the objects here. Cleanse them for Your purposes.
Remove and cut off every spirit of infirmity, bondage, fear,
divination, whoredom/idolatry, haughtiness, perverseness, anti-
Christ, deaf and dumbness, heaviness, lying, jealousy, slumber
and error. Create an atmosphere of hospitality, freedom and
comfort. Bless this room and make it a place of peace, rest and
Your lasting presence that will be a blessing to our friends and
family. In Jesus' Name. Amen.

The Bathroom

Address bathrooms in your home in the same manner that you have
other rooms. Anoint the doorways. Check out all artwork, objects and
other items that might be used by the enemy. Then pray:

Lord Jesus, break any and all demonic assignments on this
room and the objects here. Cleanse them for Your purposes.
Remove every spirit of whoredom including fornication, adultery,
molestation, rape, incest, lust, seduction, pornography,
masturbation, harlotry, illegitimacy, molestation of a child,
exhibition of the body, bestiality, perverseness and all other
sexual sins. Remove all lying spirits of condemnation, lies and
vain imaginations. Remove all attacks on identity and poor self
image spirits, including: you're ugly, worthless, stupid, you'll
never marry, no one wants you, you're trash, you'll never change,
you're fat, a whore, bitch, dummy and liar. Remove all spirits of
error and bondage that create addictions to drugs and alcohol,
and promote anorexic and bulimic behavior. Come, Holy Spirit,

and bring peace to this room. I declare that no accident will occur here. This will be a place of safety. In Jesus' Name. Amen.

The Garage

Because a garage provides another entry to the house, the prayer for this area will be one of protection. Anoint the doorway coming in and going out and the garage door itself. Also anoint each of your vehicles, including the wheels and hood area, and driver, passenger and backseat area. Then pray this prayer:

> Lord Jesus, I present this garage and entry to my home and household to You. Come and break every hex, vex, spell, evil spirit and demonic assignment from this place. Remove every spirit of infirmity, fear, divination, whoredom/idolatry, bondage, haughtiness, perverseness, deaf and dumbness, heaviness, lying, anti-Christ, stupor, error and jealousy from entering this place. I declare that You are my front and rear guard and that my household and I are protected from all assaults of the enemy. I place a hedge of protection by the blood of Jesus around this place. I declare that Your protection surrounds us everywhere each of us goes, whether at home, school, work or other activities. I declare that You are our strong tower, our refuge, our defense and a very present help in trouble. I break all assignments of accidents, injury, mishaps and death from this garage and from these vehicles. I declare that You send Your angels to watch over every member of this household, lest we dash our foot against a stone. Thank You for protection. I receive Your promises now for me and all of my household. In Jesus' Name. Amen.

Now that you have walked through the interior of your home and cleansed it, it's time to go outside, mark new boundaries and reclaim your land.

Chapter 18

Marking Boundaries

God wants to create new boundaries for your land and property and build a holy habitation for His presence. But there are often obstacles. Many different things can curse and defile the land, but there are four specific actions and activities that open the door to the demonic and create a portal for the powers of darkness. They include bloodshed from war, murder and other violence, worship of other gods or idolatry, immoral acts that bring defilement and the breaking of covenants. Certainly other things can attract the demonic, but these are the major areas Satan uses to establish curses on the land.

Bloodshed

Blood is the very essence of life. When it is shed in violence, it cries out for vengeance. Satan uses bloodshed to create an entrance into the earth. The sins of violence, murder, and the shedding of innocent blood can only be redeemed and reversed through blood.

Idolatry

God has no patience with people who worship other gods. He strictly

prohibits idolatry and those who ignore His warnings against the
exaltation and worship of false gods and their religions experience
curses. All objects that have been used in temple worship, occult
rituals or idolatry must be broken, burned and completely destroyed.

Immorality

Immorality isn't just a secret sin. It's an abomination. It gives Satan a
legal right to take possession of individual homes and capture cities. It
gives him greater access to the land and brings a spirit of defilement.

Broken Covenants

God takes His agreements seriously. His covenants are with a breach of
contract clause. So He doesn't look the other way when men break
covenants with others. In the United States and in other countries
around the world, broken treaties and other agreements have adversely
affected the land. Many lives
have been lost and blood
spilled over covenants that
were made and then broken.

> We are responsible for our homes, lands and property just as Adam and Eve were the original caretakers, landowners and authority on the Earth.

As you ask God to
reclaim your land and
property, remember you
didn't have to commit the sin
yourself to be affected by it.
God desires a heart of
repentance for what has been done by your ancestors, prior
landowners and previous tenants. As you stand in the place of
repentance and authority, you can stake the land, establish new
boundaries, receive communion, reclaim the property and create a
holy habitation for God's presence.

Now it's time to begin staking the land. Staking is an act of faith and
spiritual warfare that reclaims the land for the Lord and establishes a
border that says to the enemy, "no trespassing." We are responsible for
our homes, lands and property just as Adam and Eve were the original

caretakers, landowners and authority on the earth. God gives us the responsibility to possess the land. Stakes can be purchased in a kit or handmade. A 1-inch by 2-inch stake between 6 and 12 inches long is sufficient to drive it completely into the ground. Write scriptures on your stakes or use stakes that have scriptures already printed or inscribed on them. Bless the olive oil and rub it on each stake. You can purchase a staking kit from Vision Life Ministries.

Staking the Land

Stand together and have the head of the household make this declaration before you drive the first stake into the corner of your property.

> Lord Jesus, I repent for any and all bloodshed, idolatry, immorality, and broken covenants that have taken place on this land and property. I ask You to remove every spirit of infirmity, bondage, fear, divination, whoredom/idolatry, haughtiness, perverseness, anti-Christ, deaf and dumbness, heaviness, lying, jealousy, slumber and error that has come to this land and property for 40 generations. I ask You to break all demonic assignments and curses that have come due to these sins, transgressions and patterns of iniquity. I ask You to break all soul ties with those who have sinned and transgressed against You. I ask You to break all soul ties between every prior owner, occupant, trespasser, claimant, tenant and me and my household. I take my authority as the legal owner of this property. I set new boundary lines by the Spirit of God and say to Satan and his demonic forces that they will not cross, trespass, cage, or project onto this land, property or home. They will not bring in hexes, vexes, spells, incantations, evil spirits or assignments against me, or my household, land, property, possessions, pets or other animals. Cleanse this land by the blood of Jesus. Create new boundaries. I reclaim and set apart this home, land and property for Your use and Yours alone. In Jesus' Name. Amen.

Take the first stake and drive it into the north corner of your property at the legal boundary line. Read out loud the Scriptures written on all sides of the stakes. Pour some additional oil over the stake and around the corner area of the boundary line. Do the same at each corner of your land until you have placed one stake at the remaining east, south and west corners. Walk the property line and pour out anointing oil while you say Scriptures to reclaim the land. The next step in the process is communion.

An Everlasting Sign

In preparing for communion, remember that there is no greater reality for the believer, than the blood sacrifice of Jesus. His body and His blood are the everlasting sign of our covenant. When Jesus observed the Passover meal with His disciples before His betrayal, trial and death on the Cross, He spoke volumes to them and to us about its meaning. Passover comes from the Hebrew word "pasah" which means to "hop, skip over or spare." It refers directly to God's passing over of the children of Israel in Egypt because the blood was sprinkled on the doorposts of their homes.

> There is no greater reality for the believer, than the blood sacrifice of Jesus.

While death killed the firstborn of every Egyptian household, the first child of every Hebrew slept safely in their beds. God came as the Deliverer. So Jesus comes to us as the One Who delivers from sin, sickness, demons, fear and death. He is the One Who provides freedom and life for every captive.

The Cups of the Passover

To the believer, the blood of Jesus represents full redemption through His sinless sacrifice which cleanses us from all sin and gives us a place of authority as a joint heir. Even though we drink only one cup, at Passover the Jews drank five.

The first cup is sanctification. Set yourself and your household apart for Him. The second cup is judgment. He has paid the price for your sins. Allow the Spirit of God to remove every judgment on your house and every plague of the enemy that goes with it. The third is the cup of blessing. Receive the blessing of being a child of God and joint heir with Jesus Christ for you and your household. Open your arms and take the blessings of 1,000 godly generations that come to you as you choose to serve the Lord.

The fourth cup is praise. When God delivers you and your household, make sure that you and those gathered with you praise God for what He has done. The fifth cup is the blessing of the Messiah. For you as a believer who has already received the Anointed One, Jesus Christ, this last cup provides a daily opportunity to open the door of your house to Jesus and create a continual portal every day for His presence.

Observing Communion

Now it's time to take communion. As I mentioned earlier, your particular theological point of view may differ from mine regarding communion and I respect those differences. Feel free to observe and practice only what you are comfortable with. God will honor your obedience and cleanse your land.

Get some fruit of the vine as the symbol of the blood of Jesus, and an unbroken loaf of bread as the symbol of His body. Gather your family and friends together and find the center of your property. Take the remaining oil that was not used during the staking process and pour a circle around the group. Then have everyone step inside the circle. Pray these prayers as you take communion in remembrance of your unbreakable, eternal covenant with God through Jesus Christ.

Remembering Your Covenant

Provide an unbroken loaf of bread. Have each person tear off a piece from the loaf and pass it to the next person. Keep the rest of the loaf. When everyone has their bread, pray this:

Receiving the Bread

Thank You, Lord Jesus, for Your body that was given as a complete and perfect sacrifice for me, my household and all who have gathered here today. Thank You for the wholeness it brings to each of us, to our spirit, soul—mind, will and emotions—and body. Thank You for the grief and sorrow You bore, the wounds and bruises You took, the sickness You received and the sin You became. Because of Your sacrifice, each of us can receive shalom—wholeness, soundness, with nothing missing and nothing broken. We take this bread, the bread of Your body given for us, with a grateful heart for all it has purchased for us. We receive Your body as a sacrifice for us now. (Eat the bread).

For the entire cleansing process you will need several quarts of the fruit of the vine. For communion, provide one large glass and have each person take a drink and pass it to the next person. Once every person has their drink, pray this prayer:

Receiving the Blood of Jesus

Thank You, Lord Jesus, for Your blood which was given as a complete and perfect sacrifice for my sins and those of my household and all who have gathered here today. Thank You for the total redemption, cleansing, wholeness, and right-standing that it brings with You. Thank You that it brings deliverance and freedom. It removes all the strongholds of the enemy on each of us, spirit, soul—mind, will and emotions—and body. That it brings healing—physical, emotional—and makes us sound and stable. That it makes right that which was wrong between us and puts us in right-standing with You as joint heirs with Jesus Christ. That gives us authority to speak and act in Your Name. We take this symbol of Your blood, the fruit of the vine, with a grateful heart for all that You purchased for us. We receive Your blood as the perfect sacrifice for us now.

If the following suggestion is not consistent with your beliefs about the elements of the Lord's Supper, you may choose not to complete this portion of the cleansing. If, however, you wish to continue, do the following. Dig a hole for the fruit of the vine and the bread left over from communion. Once the hole has been dug, place the remaining portion of the unbroken loaf of bread in the hole. Pour a large portion of the fruit of the vine over the bread. Cover the elements with dirt. Then use the remaining fruit of the vine to pour a circle around the group. When you are finished, step back into the circle. Now make this declaration:

> By the authority of the Name of Jesus and by His shed blood and broken body, I reclaim and redeem this land. I declare that by the Spirit of God, it is holy ground, sanctified and cleansed, set apart for the presence and glory of God, and Him alone. Amen.

At the conclusion of the prayer, begin to create a canopy of praise (sing out loud songs of praise until the presence of God comes in the circle) to God for all that He has done to deliver your home and land, and release it forever from the captivity of darkness and the evil one. As you worship Him, you will prepare an atmosphere for His Spirit to come and open a lasting portal to His presence.

Chapter 19

A Glorious Habitation

Proverbs 3:33 says, "The curse of the Lord is on the house of the wicked, But He blesses the home of the just." Now that God has cleansed your home and land, it is imperative that you maintain an atmosphere for God's presence and allow Him to make your home and land a holy habitation.

God's desire has always been to be close to His people. Under the Old Covenant He revealed His presence in the wilderness through the pillar of fire at night and the column of smoke by day. He showed His glory above the Ark of the Covenant. He spoke through kings, prophets and judges who proclaimed His message to the people. He met the high priest and released His presence in the holy of holies at the temple. It wasn't until the new covenant, however, that God brought His presence by the Holy Spirit into the life of every believer. We have become a dwelling place where He can live and move by His Spirit.

For All the World to See

Wherever we go and whatever we do, the Spirit of God goes with us and affects the world around us. We are the fragrance and knowledge of Him spoken of in 2 Corinthians 2:14. So it is critically important that our lives, homes and land be dedicated and set apart for God's power and presence to operate. Allow your home and all that surrounds it to be a refuge and a holy habitation for God's continual presence. Let your home be a place of shelter, protection, peace and rest. Make sure that over the days, months and years ahead, you keep your home free from demonic spirits.

You can do several things to keep Satan and the forces of darkness far from your household. First, make sure that you keep anything out of your home that would bring an unholy presence into your household. Second, continue to consecrate and set aside your home and land to God. Third, honor God with attitudes, an atmosphere and activities that bring Him glory. Fourth, stay spiritually alert against the attacks of the enemy and exercise your spiritual authority in the Name of Jesus. Fifth, confront ungodly attitudes and values, and deal with evil before it establishes a foothold and builds a stronghold. Sixth, keep strife, discord and division from your relationships, and resolve differences quickly. Seventh, establish a godly heritage for your children.

As you do these things day by day, I believe that your home will become a beacon of light in the darkness and a refuge in time of trouble for those around you. We are living in the times when the dramatic differences between light and darkness are getting more and more obvious. Those individuals, families, neighborhoods, cities, states and even countries which today choose righteousness will arise, shine and be great lights of God's glory. His holy habitation will be seen in the years and decades that lie ahead.

> Arise, shine; For your light has come! And the glory of the Lord is risen upon you. For behold, the darkness shall cover the earth, and deep darkness the people; But the Lord will arise over you, And His glory will be seen upon you.
>
> Isaiah 60:1-3

About the Author

Dr. Henry Malone, co-founder of Vision Life Ministries, is sounding the battle cry for freedom everywhere. Formerly a senior pastor of 28 years, with 44 years of combined ministry background, Henry is bringing the message of deliverance and inner healing to churches, ministries, pastors, families and individuals.

Since 1989, his commitment to bring freedom to the captives and healing to the brokenhearted has sent him to cities all across the United States and around the world proclaiming and demonstrating the works of the kingdom of God. Henry presents Freedom and Fullness Seminars and releases the ministry of Jesus in groups and one on one to bring healing, deliverance and freedom.

Since 1992, Henry has trained, equipped and released interns for ministry in the areas of deliverance and emotional healing. In 1998, he established the School of Deliverance Ministry to help local churches bring victory to those experiencing the bondage of demonic oppression and the pain of emotional trauma. Each year, Henry also helps train pastors in third-world nations and travels to churches and conferences speaking on behalf of world missions.

Henry and his wife, Tina, have two grown children, four grandchildren and live in Grand Prairie, Texas.

Index

altars 34

ancestors 28

authority 5, 8, 9, 12, 17-18, 24, 33,
    48-49, 53, 58, 70, 80, 98-99,
    103, 108, 111, 124, 136-140,
    143-144, 152-160

Babylon 9, 87, 90, 115

blessing 7, 19, 48, 69, 98-100, 117,
    137, 143-145, 148, 155

blood 5, 7, 11, 19-20, 32-34, 41, 50,
    52-53, 57-66, 97, 103-131, 137,
    140, 144, 147, 149, 151-157

bloodshed 59, 65, 104, 151, 153

bondage 51, 78, 86, 117, 118, 120,
    144-149, 153

captives 52, 114, 118

cleansing 5, 16, 24, 27, 35, 44, 53,
    104, 106, 115, 128-132, 135,
    140, 143-144, 156

coven 6

covenant 19, 48, 51-53, 62, 87-88, 97-
    104, 106, 108, 121, 136, 146,
    151-155, 159

creation 31, 32, 39, 51-53, 69-70, 85-
    87, 98-99, 117, 136

curses 25, 27, 47, 48, 55, 58, 64, 99,
    115, 137, 151-153

deception 82, 100

defilement 35, 82, 116, 128-131, 151-
    152

deliverance 26, 44, 53, 73, 107, 108,
    112, 117, 156

disobedience vi, 41, 48, 50-51, 59, 99,
    112-113, 116

dominion 33, 49, 69-70, 98, 99

fellowship 31-32, 35, 144

freedom 3, 21, 57, 82, 107-108, 114,
    118, 125, 148, 154, 156

freemasonry 28, 80, 115

generational curses 8, 41, 59

generations 33, 51, 63, 153, 155

habitation 10, 18, 20-21, 31-35, 140-141, 144, 151-152, 159-160

Halloween 41, 91, 92

Harry Potter 16, 39

haunted 58, 92

heal 29, 53, 106, 111, 116-117, 130, 144, 156

high place 37, 85-89, 93

idolatry 27, 35, 72, 77, 80-82, 85-87, 89, 91, 93, 113, 115, 128-129, 144, 146-153

idols 78, 80, 82, 85, 90, 93

iniquity 59, 61, 62, 66, 72, 105, 113, 129, 132, 153

inner vow 8

intimacy 31, 32, 35, 93, 146, 147

land 4, 7-12, 33, 41, 44, 50, 52, 58-60, 65, 69, 86, 88, 104, 116-119, 128-129, 137, 140-141, 143, 149, 151-160

liberty 51, 118

new covenant 19, 33, 53, 104, 159

pets 106, 107, 137-141, 153

Pokemon 16, 25, 39

portal 34, 37, 39, 41-44, 64, 151, 155, 157

possessions 4, 10, 12, 27, 35, 44, 80, 106, 117-119, 124, 131, 137, 140-141, 143, 153

power 7-8, 19-21, 25, 35, 37, 39, 53, 71, 74, 78, 80, 9-93, 105, 108, 109, 119, 121, 124, 129, 137-140, 144, 151, 160

property 3-12, 18, 35, 37, 41, 64-65, 106, 117-121, 131, 140, 141, 143, 151-155

protection 19-21, 35, 42, 43, 111-112, 118, 144-145, 148-149, 160

rebellion 32-35, 49-50, 70, 87, 112-116, 136

redemption 53, 104, 106, 117-120, 125, 154, 156

renounce 137

repentance 11, 112-117, 152

restitution 33, 120-123

restoration 33, 106, 121-124

rituals 6, 27-28, 88, 91, 115, 152

root spirits 25

sacrifice 5, 34, 52, 63, 65, 74, 88-89, 99, 104-105, 114-115, 136, 154-156

shekinah 33

sorcery 92

supernatural 38-40, 64, 130

trauma 8, 16, 41

Wicca 91

Freedom and Fullness Seminars

This two-day seminar is an in-depth look at the 2-5-14 strategy introduced in Dr. Henry Malone's book *Shadow Boxing*. Specifically designed to lead a church or group through corporate deliverance, the seminar begins on Friday night and continues through late Saturday afternoon. The seminar includes both intensive teaching and ministry time and includes an extensive workbook. A teaching and ministry team that has been trained or is in the process of being trained by Vision Life Ministries leads each seminar.

The seminar teaching includes the following topics:

▶ The War of the Ages
▶ Proclaiming Liberty
▶ Two Ways Satan Gains Ground: Intrusion and Legal Ground
▶ The Five Doors: Disobedience, Inner Vows, Curses, Emotional Trauma, Unforgiveness
▶ Strongholds and Root Spirits
▶ How to Break Curses and Tear Down Strongholds
▶ How to Walk in Freedom

For churches interested in more information regarding this exciting and life-changing seminar, please contact:

Vision Life Ministries
P.O. Box 153691
Irving, TX 75015
(972) 206-2419
www.visionlife.org

Personal Ministry Training

The Personal Ministry Training will encourage, train and equip those who desire wholeness in their own lives and/or desire to extend the Kingdom of God through ministering deliverance and inner healing. After participating in this three-part training school, a person will be prepared to lead personal ministry sessions.

PERSONAL MINISTRY TRAINING ONE develops the strategy of the warrior and focuses on training for leading personal ministry sessions. Some of the major subjects covered are:

- Scriptural Basis for Deliverance
- Authority of the Believer
- 2-5-14 Strategy for Deliverance
- Healing the Brokenhearted
- Weapons of Our Warfare
- Learning to Listen
- How to Interview
- The Ongoing Nature of Deliverance
- Actual Demonstration of a Deliverance Session Using the 2-5-14 Strategy

PERSONAL MINISTRY TRAINING TWO develops the heart of the warrior and focuses on the attitudes and character necessary to be fruitful and effective in life and ministry. Some of the subjects covered are:

- Shattering the Foundation of Rebellion
- Dealing with Mother/Father Wounds
- Changing the Cause of Prolonged Pain
- Removing Shame
- Recovering Identity
- Disconnecting from Witchcraft
- Overcoming Codependency
- Developing a Pure Heart
- Anointing of the Warrior
- Confidentiality
- Sexual Integrity and Much More

(Continued on next page)

PERSONAL MINISTRY TRAINING THREE develops the gifts and skills of the warrior. It focuses on demonstration and participation in actual personal deliverance sessions. During the course of these two and one half days, the students will be engaged in several actual full deliverance sessions using the 2-5-14 strategy of deliverance and inner healing.

This hands-on involvement in the exercising of their discerning abilities, testing of their spiritual authority, utilizing their listening and interview skills and increasing of their anointing completes the three-part training school. A person will be prepared to lead personal ministry sessions upon completion of the Personal Ministry Training.

Vision Life Ministries
P.O. Box 153691
Irving, TX 75015
(972) 206-2419
www.visionlife.org

Order Form

You may place an order for product using any of the following:

- Call to place your order: **(972) 206-2419**
- Postal orders: **Vision Life Ministries, P.O. Box 153691, Irving, TX 75015**
- Order online at **www.visionlife.org**

Title	Price	Quantity		Amount
Portals to Cleansing	$12	x _____	=	_____
Portals to Cleansing Kit	$12	x _____	=	_____
Shadow Boxing	$12	x _____	=	_____
Islam Unmasked	$10	x _____	=	_____

Shipping and Handling _____
(Please add $6 for the first book and $2 for each additional book)

Total _____

____ Please send more information about Freedom and Fullness seminars.

____ Please send more information about Personal Ministry Training.

Name (Please print clearly)

Address   Apt.

City   State   ZIP

Country   Phone

E-Mail

Method of Payment
____Check/Money Order (Payable to Vision Life Ministries) ____VISA ____MasterCard

Card Number   Expiration Date

Card Holder (Please print clearly)

Signature